W9-CFD-469

THE
MEANING
OF
DREAMS

THE
MEANING
OF
DREAMS

by Franklin D. Martini

GRAMERCY BOOKS
New York

Copyright © 2000 by Ottenheimer Publishers, Inc.

All rights reserved under International and Pan-American
Copyright Conventions.

No part of this book may be reproduced or transmitted in any form or by any
means electronic or mechanical including photocopying, recording, or any
information storage and retrieval system, without permission in writing
from the publisher.

This 2000 edition is published by Gramercy Books™,
an imprint of Random House Value Publishing, Inc.
280 Park Avenue, New York, NY 10017
by arrangement with Ottenheimer Publishers, Inc.
5 Park Center Court, Suite 300, Owings Mills, MD 21117.

Gramercy Books™ and design are trademarks of
Random House Value Publishing, Inc.

Random House
New York • Toronto • London • Sydney • Auckland
http://www.randomhouse.com/

Printed and bound in the United States of America.

A catalog record for this title is available from the Library of Congress.

ISBN: 0-517-16250-4

9 8 7 6 5 4 3 2 1

Table of Contents

Foreword

Since ancient times, people have put great faith in dreams, believing them to be visions that can forewarn us of good fortune or bad luck.

Today, it is common knowledge that dreams do indeed pertain symbolically to events or problems happening in the dreamer's life. Dreams can actually offer fascinating insight to help us solve our problems, and we can often help people close to us as well.

The late Franklin D. Martini was a psychologist, astrologer, palm reader, handwriting expert, and master interpreter of dreams. He spent a lifetime unlocking the meanings behind our dreams.

In his day, Martini was a familiar name in the homes of those who believed in the occult sciences. He wrote many books and enjoyed the devotion of many ardent followers.

In *The Meaning of Dreams*, Martini—along with another author and expert who wished to remain anonymous—has listed the most common dreams and given his interpretations. We have modernized the language, without changing the explanations.

Martini was convinced that life is an eternal spiritual journey. He viewed dreams as messages from the soul. These entries are shared in the hope that they may guide you on your own journey.

The Publisher

A

"Dreams take us to levels we would otherwise be afraid to strive for."

BILL BEHAM, American entrepreneur

Abbot

To dream of an abbot in a monastery as a happy scene implies that you are gaining much from following your inner counsel. If the scene is grim or not a happy one, you are warned to contemplate your life lest you lose your spirituality.

Abdomen

To dream that you see this part of your body foretells that your greatest expectation will be realized, providing you redouble your energies on your labors instead of toward pleasure. Should you dream that this part of your body is sunken or shriveled, it foretells that you will be persecuted by false friends. To see your abdomen protruding or swollen signifies trials and tribulations that may be conquered by determined efforts on your part.

Abortion

For a woman to dream that she is undergoing this procedure

is an indication that some scandal is hanging in her immediate future. For a physician to dream that he is involved in an abortion foretells troubles to the dreamer brought about through lack of attention to duties.

Abscess
To dream that you are suffering with such an affliction denotes that your misfortunes are likely to overwhelm you.

Abuse
To dream of abusing an individual foretells bad luck in your daily affairs. You are likely to lose money through the influence of others who may induce you to act against your will. To dream that someone abuses you foretells that you will be mistreated in your daily affairs.

Abyss
To dream of falling into an abyss implies feeling a loss of control over some area of one's self or life. It would be advisable to gather strength and courage, and do what it takes to reassert control.

Accident
To dream of such a misfortune is a warning to avoid any form of travel, at least for the immediate time, because your life may be in danger.

Accusation
To dream that you are accusing someone shows unexpressed anger. Find a way to express it constructively, lest it fester and

bring on an illness. To dream of being accused of something, rightly or wrongly, suggests that you will soon confront an unpleasant situation. Staying calm in the face of the accusation is advisable.

Aches

To dream of such symptoms foretells that you are too frank and open in your business dealings, and that others will profit by your ideas.

Acorn

To dream of an acorn shows that you could begin something that appears trivial but will, in the long term, reap many rewards.

Acquaintance

To dream that you meet an acquaintance and the meeting results in a fuss or argument denotes a division in your family, infidelity in love, or perhaps business losses.

Actor or Actress

To dream that you are in this profession denotes that there is much hard work before you, but by persevering, your ambitions will be realized. For a woman to dream that she is to marry an actor denotes that her ambitions will be thwarted. If a married man dreams that he is involved with an actress, this means family troubles. If the man is single, it represents friction with his sweetheart.

Adoption

If a childless couple dreams of adopting children, this portends that a child will soon enter their lives. For others, a dream of an adoption signifies acquiring new responsibilities by circumstance, rather than by choice.

Adultery

To dream that you have perpetrated this act is, in most cases, a bad omen. Should the person you dream of be married, you can be sure that some trouble or misfortune is about to confront you. If a virgin dreams of adultery, this indicates an early invitation to a wedding. When a married woman dreams of adultery, it signifies that she will soon conceive, and is a strong sign that it will be a girl. If a single woman dreams of adultery, this denotes troubles and obstacles for her. If a man dreams that he has had an opportunity to commit adultery and was unable to perpetrate the act through some physical inability, this denotes a rival or competitor in business, and sometimes an illness.

Affliction

To dream that you see a friend suffering with an injury or affliction denotes the receipt of money or good news.

Afraid

To dream that you are afraid to go ahead with some project tells of discontent in your household, and the prospect that business may suffer.

Agony

To feel agony as you dream is not a good sign; this foretells of weariness and pleasure, the former likely to predominate. To dream that you are in agony over monetary affairs is a sign that you will hear of the illness of a close friend.

Air

To dream that you are inhaling hot air is a sign that you will be influenced against your will. Cold air denotes a decline in business and, in turn, will bring family troubles.

Alley

To dream of a dark alley suggests that the path you are setting upon will lead to trouble. To dream of starting down a well lit alley, as a shortcut, suggests that you could streamline some activities.

Alligator

To dream that you see an alligator crawling is a sign that you must exercise much care in any new step that you may be contemplating.

Almonds

To dream of seeing or eating almonds signifies difficulty and trouble.

Alms

To dream that you are asked to give alms, and you refuse to

do so, shows that want and misery will befall you; but to dream that you give freely is a sign of great joy and long life.

Almshouse
To dream of this institution is indicative that one's marriage will not be a solid one.

Altar
To dream of an altar predicts joy and gladness.

Amorous
To dream that you feel amorous will lead you toward a scandal.

Anchor
To see an anchor denotes that your hope is not in vain.

Angels
To dream of these heavenly messengers relates to a changed condition in the near future. This tells of good news and a possible legacy not far away.

Anger
To see an angry person act in a manner that is unjust or negative suggests you have a temper that needs to be reined in. However, if the anger is justified, this is encouragement for you to express anger that has been held back.

Antelope

To see wild antelope and deer, in a wood or on a hillside, reflects a longing to get away from present circumstances. You are advised to either rest or take a vacation. To see an antelope or a deer slain signifies disillusionment to come.

Antique

To see a rare object or a work of art hints that your own uniqueness can be used to your advantage, and that you should take pride in it.

Ants

To dream of these little pests foretells of many trifling annoyances in your daily doings that will tire you without accomplishing much of anything.

Anvil

To dream of an anvil in a blacksmith's shop suggests that success and honor will be achieved despite any opposition.

Apes

To dream of apes is an omen of sickness and disease. To see an ape in a tree means that the dreamer is warned to be careful of false and deceitful friends.

Apparel

For a man to dream of women's apparel denotes trouble or temptations of some kind caused by a woman. If the apparel is flashy, illicit cohabitation may take place.

Apples

To dream of apples is an excellent omen. To see apples on trees tells of prosperity. To eat them, if they are good and ripe, is a signal for you to go ahead and carry out your plans.

Apricots

To dream of apricots in season denotes contentment, health, and pleasure. If the apricots are out of season or not yet ripe, this signifies vain hopes and a poor outcome for a project.

Apron

To dream of an apron foretells of an uneven course. For a woman to lose an apron foretells censure and criticism from elders.

Arch

To see an arch in a doorway or building is an omen of good fortune. To pass under an arch denotes new beginnings in better circumstances.

Architect

To dream of an architect drawing up blueprints indicates that careful planning will benefit you at this time. All details should be accounted for in order to achieve maximum success.

Arms

To dream that your arms are strong and muscular is a sign that you can succeed in your ventures. If you dream that your arms are hairy, this signifies an upcoming turn towards prosperity. To dream that your right arm is cut off signifies the loss of a valued friendship due to a terrible quarrel, or by death.

Army

To see an army fighting denotes great conflict in your life. If the army is victorious, relief is at hand. If not, you must continue to bear the circumstances.

Arrest

To see someone arrested denotes a need to stop doing something, lest it bring unwanted consequences. To arrest someone in a dream implies that you will put an end to someone else's dishonesty.

Arrows

To dream that others are shooting arrows into your body denotes that a pending suspicion will be verified.

Ascend

To dream that you are ascending to some high point, but experience trouble in reaching it, foretells of disappointment.

Assassin

To dream that you receive a blow from an assassin means you will be disappointed in your efforts. To see blood in any form caused by the assassin is a sign of enemies endeavoring to destroy your conditions.

Attack

To dream of being attacked suggests that you feel vulnerable and need to say "no" to others more often.

Aunt

To dream of your aunt is a sign that you will receive a reprimand for an action you are not guilty of.

Authority

It is always a good omen to dream that you are in a position of authority.

Automobile

To dream that you are riding in an automobile denotes that you will be restless and regret some deed or act you have committed.

B

"I believe it to be true that dreams are the true interpreters of our inclinations; but there is art required to sort and understand them."

MONTAIGNE, French essayist

Baby

To dream that you hear a baby crying is a sign of disappointment and sickness. To dream of a bright, healthy baby denotes success in love and many warm friends. To dream of a sickly baby tells of many difficulties.

Bachelor

For a single man to dream that he is enjoying bachelorhood to the fullest is a warning for the dreamer to keep away from matrimony, for the present at least, because desperate, designing women want to marry him. However, if the dream of being a bachelor is an unhappy one, this means you are ready for commitment and should propose to the woman in your life. If a married man dreams of being a bachelor, this denotes that the temptations of other women are becoming a problem.

Back

To dream of a broken back shows that you are undertaking too many responsibilities. If the back is hurt or scarred, this indicates a need to take your responsibilities more seriously. To dream of a strong backbone signifies health and joy.

Bacon

To dream you are eating bacon is considered good; rancid bacon tells of worries and difficulties.

Badge

To dream of wearing a badge or identification denotes a need to speak up more.

Bagpipes

To dream of playing bagpipes signifies trouble and contention.

Bakery

To dream of being in a bakery, but not buying anything, suggests that you are eating too many baked goods or starches. To dream of buying well baked goods in a bakery is a signal that there will soon be cause to rejoice.

Baking

For a woman to dream of baking is not a good sign; it speaks of illness and the care of a large family that may depend on her for support. To see yourself baking and enjoying it foretells of a successful venture that many will take part in and enjoy. If the baked goods do not turn out well, this warns of trouble in a venture and a poor outcome, unless steps are taken immediately to alter its course. To dream of baking bread using yeast suggests that you are working on something that will influence many. You are advised to be patient and to persevere.

Bald

To dream that you see a man with a bald head tells that enemies are trying to injure you in your interests; by persevering you will outwit their efforts and be justly rewarded.

Ball (Dance)

To dream that you see others or yourself at a great ball signifies joy and pleasure. If you dream of this regularly, this indicates a need for more recreation in your life.

Ball (Sports Object)

To dream of playing with a ball means you have a skill that you can bring to fruition. To do marvelous things with a ball in a dream signifies great success with ideas you are harboring.

Balloon

To dream of seeing a balloon is a sign of a potential slump in business. To go up in a balloon means an unpleasant trip is in the offing.

Banana

To dream of a banana denotes that you are likely to marry someone of very poor character and that you will be unhappy.

To dream of eating bananas tells of friction in business. To see overripe or rotten bananas tells of an undertaking that will be distasteful to you.

Bandits

To dream of being attacked by bandits is a warning to guard your own safety and the safety of your home. Or, if your home and personal habits are safe ones, this dream implies that you feel imposed upon, and denotes a need to set more boundaries with others. To attack bandits who cross your path means you have to use healthy assertiveness in your life to remove obstacles.

Banjo

To dream of this instrument foretells a merry time for you in the near future. To see another playing a banjo tells of slight worries that will soon fade away.

Bank

To see a bank without officers in your dream is an omen of business losses. To see the tellers pay out money tells of some careless act on your part.

Banker

To dream of a banker signifies a need to examine your financial habits.

Bankruptcy

To dream of being bankrupt is a dire warning regarding financial circumstances and spending habits. However, this can also portend spiritual bankruptcy, if you are abandoning early moral training.

Banquets

To dream of a banquet indicates opportunities that will bring prosperity.

Baptism

To dream you are being baptized signifies you will be saved from a difficult circumstance.

Bar

To dream that you are mixing drinks behind a bar denotes a desire to cover your actions by deceptive plans.

Barbarian

To struggle with a barbarian implies a temptation you need to resist.

Barber

To dream of a barber denotes that success and happiness will come to you after you have endured much hard work. For a woman to dream of a barber is a sign that her fortune will come very slowly and that patience is needed.

Barefoot

To dream you are barefoot, but walking happily, indicates a new sense of freedom is about to enter your life. However, if the ground is covered with material that can injure the foot, this denotes a difficult period and the need to tread carefully, especially with superiors.

Barking
To dream of dogs barking signifies insults and gossip from competitors. If you scare the dogs away, you will triumph over your competitors.

Barn
To dream you are in an empty barn foretells that you will find a marriage confining. To dream of a barn filled with grain or cattle foretells progress in a career.

Barrel
To see a full barrel signifies abundance; if empty, it predicts a period of poverty.

Baseball
To dream of baseball tells that you will cultivate contentment and become a cheerful companion. To dream that you are playing baseball tells that you will enjoy much pleasure in the near future.

Basket
To dream of a full basket denotes good fortune; an empty one suggests disappointment and loneliness.

Bath
To dream that you need a bath is a signal that something you

are hiding is about to come to light. If the bathwater is too hot, someone in authority will ask you to account for something done poorly. If you have not yet entered the bath, the trouble is of short duration. If the water is too cold, you will encounter resistance to future plans. If the temperature is just right and you enjoy your bath, you are about to enter a happy period in your life.

Bathing

To dream that you are bathing in clear water is a sign of good fortune. To bathe in warm water is generally a sign of some trouble. To go bathing with others is an omen that you must be careful in the selection of your companions. To see people bathing in such perfectly clear water that you can see the actions of their bodies relates to honor and distinction. To dream that you are bathing yourself foretells that you will offer a kindness to some person who will be thankful.

Bathtub

To dream of a bathtub filled with water implies the need to immerse yourself in something such as studies or work, and that doing so will leave your life in better shape than it was before.

Bats

It is a bad omen to dream of bats; it foretells troubles, sickness, and even death.

Battle

To engage in battle predicts conflict. If the end of the dream shows tactful conversation, this implies that the conflict can be avoided or resolved through proper and positive communication.

Beads

To see a beautiful string of beads on an attractive woman denotes that persistence and patience in work will bring satisfaction and rewards.

Beans

To dream of beans is not good. To see them grow is a sign of illness. Dried beans mean disappointment in material things. To eat beans signifies bad news from loved ones.

Bear

To dream of this animal is a sign of great competition in pursuits of every kind. To dream of killing a bear is a sign that you will be able to overcome your difficulties.

Beard

To see a long beard predicts long life and health. To see a black beard that is not well-trimmed implies troubles from a man. A red beard indicates success through energetic application, and is an encouragement to strike while the iron is hot in a present business prospect.

Beauty

To dream of beauty is an excellent omen. To dream of a beautiful woman symbolizes peace, harmony, and success in business as well as in love.

Bed

To dream that a bed is clean and neat tells of worries ending. If you dream that you are in a strange bed, it is a sign of unexpected friends who will visit you soon.

Bedbug

To dream of bedbugs suggests difficulties in your romantic relationships.

Beef

To dream of raw beef is an omen that bodily pain may be in store for you; therefore, it is advisable to use good common sense before proceeding. To eat beef that is pleasing to the taste means gains in business.

Beehive

To see a beehive denotes a busy period ahead, but one that will bring much success.

Beer

To drink beer means disappointment. To see others drink means someone will reveal your dishonest scheme.

Bees

To dream of these busy little creatures foretells a profitable undertaking. It would be well for the dreamer to act at once to take advantage of opportunity.

Beetles

To see beetles crawling on you denotes poor luck. To kill them is a good omen.

Beets

To dream of eating beets signifies freedom from trouble, and upcoming success in a career.

Beggar

To dream of a beggar is a sign of poor business, generally caused by poor management. To give to a beggar tells that you will soon be satisfied with your surroundings and will live in peace and contentment.

Bells

To dream of church bells ringing is an omen that good news will soon arrive. To dream of alarm bells is a sign that upsetting news will soon come.

Belly

To dream of stomach trouble, if you are in good health, denotes troubles in your career or in a relationship. If the state of health is unknown, this suggests you should get a medical checkup. For a man to dream of a large belly is a warning of health problems. For a woman to dream of a large belly refers to success in an undertaking, or foretells the birth of a child.

Belt

To dream that there is a belt around you is a sign that you are going to meet a stranger who will create a good deal of gossip about you.

Bet

To dream that you are betting on games of chance is a sign to be cautious in new undertakings. Unscrupulous competitors are trying to divert your attention in an illegitimate direction. Furthermore, it is a sign that others are trying to wring money from you by some cunning device.

Bible

To dream of this holy book denotes that some innocent act will be turned into unexpected happiness.

Bill

To dream of paying a bill denotes good luck to come. To dream of a bill that you are unable to pay foretells financial problems.

Birds

It is a favorable omen to dream of birds. If their plumage is beautiful, a wealthy and happy partner will be yours. To see birds flying denotes prosperity to the dreamer. To catch birds is a good omen. To hear them speak denotes a work assignment that requires much caution. To kill birds tells of misfortune.

Bird's Nest

To dream of finding a bird's nest is a sign of some special surprise about to cross your path. But if the nest is without either eggs or birds, you will meet with disappointment for something anticipated.

Birth

For a woman to dream of giving birth is an omen of an actual child to come, if she wishes one. Otherwise, this indicates the beginning of something precious and beautiful in your life, but which will need much attention and care.

Birth (Premature)

For a woman to dream that she gives birth prematurely denotes that her very next child will be bright and achieve excellent grades in school. If a childless woman dreams of a premature birth, she will achieve success in her ambitions.

Bite

To dream that something bites you is a sign of much work ahead; also, some indirect losses are threatened.

Blacksmith

To dream that you are a blacksmith foretells hard work. To see a blacksmith at work denotes success.

Blanket

To dream of a soiled blanket signifies treachery. If nice and clean, it signifies success and an illness averted through exercised caution.

Bleeding

To dream that you are bleeding tells of misfortune or possible death, and also of the possibility of many things turning against you.

Blind

To dream of blind people foretells that someone will ask you for financial aid. To dream you are afflicted with blindness tells that a great change is about to overtake you—probably from the height of success to the pit of poverty.

Blister

To see a blister on your hand suggests that you are unprepared for the tasks in front of you.

Blood

To dream that you see blood flowing from a wound tells of physical ailment and much worry.

Blossoms

To see trees or flowers in blossom in your dream is a sign of peace and success in the near future, and the beginning of a period in your life that will bring peace and prosperity.

Blushing

To dream you are blushing denotes that you will be troubled over a false accusation. To see others blush tells of some blunder that was caused by an embarrassing act of yours.

Boa Constrictor

To see a boa constrictor in a dream warns you to beware of unexpected verbal attacks from associates.

Boar

To dream that a wild boar is running towards you in a forest indicates unexpected trouble. If the boar changes course or is standing still, the trouble is avoidable.

Boast

To see someone boasting in a dream is a warning not to take someone too seriously. If you see yourself boasting in a dream, this implies that you need to respect others' abilities as much as your own.

Boat

To dream you are in a boat on a river, lake, or pond is a good sign, and denotes joyous feelings, prosperity, and success. If the water is muddy, past indiscretions will come back to haunt you. If the water is rough, you are entering a difficult period in your life; but it will not last.

Bodyguard

To dream of a bodyguard suggests that whatever has been troubling you will soon subside.

Boils

To see a boil on a face means that the angry attitudes you are harboring are creating problems. To see a boil on a back denotes responsibilities that are not being handled well.

Bones

To dream of seeing a lot of bones is a sign of bad influences around you.

Bookcase

To dream of an empty bookcase indicates that something needs to be learned before progress can come. A full bookcase indicates you need to share what you've learned with others.

Books

To dream of finding a book you enjoy reading denotes you will discover new learning that will be exciting. To see a room full of books that are appealing denotes further learning that will open new horizons. To see a book gathering dust suggests unused talents that could be of help. To dream of studying books is a sign of honor and riches. To dream of old books is a sign to keep away from evil. To dream of hunting for books foretells troubles.

Boots

To dream of old boots indicates an illness and displeasure. New boots denote luck in your dealings and a possible raise in salary for your labors.

Borrowing

To borrow money in a dream foretells of a shortage soon to befall. If someone borrows from you, this warns of a possible loss of goods, unless you take care.

Bottles

To dream of bottles that are filled with some transparent fluid is an elegant omen of prosperity in business and conquest in love.

Bowling Alley
To be in an empty bowling alley suggests you need to take a more playful attitude towards life. To be bowling with others suggests that cooperation brings rewards.

Box
To dream of opening a full box tells of riches and delightful journeys. To dream of opening an empty box tells of disappointment and hardship.

Bracelet
To dream that you are wearing a bracelet on your arm, possibly a gift from a sweetheart, indicates that you may marry early.

Brain
To see a healthy brain is a sign of wisdom. If the brain shows deterioration or imperfections, this implies a need to accept your limitations.

Brandy
To dream of a glass of brandy sipped with pleasure foretells of a successful endeavor.

Bread
To dream of seeing a lot of bread is an omen of peace and plenty throughout life.

Breakfast
To dream of eating breakfast indicates a new beginning or a new cycle in life.

26

Breaking

To dream of breaking something is a signal that either you or someone around you is exerting too much force in handling something, which will lead to its destruction. This is a warning to ease up.

Breasts

To see firm and shapely breasts is an indication of healing powers.

Brewery

To dream of a brewery signifies distractions that can undo your career.

Bricks

To dream of a brick foretells unsettled business and troubles in love. To see bricks in high piles signifies many talents that, if applied, will lead to success. To see a house built of bricks is an indication of a solid marriage and home life.

Bride

For a young woman to dream that she is a bride is a sign of money by inheritance, which will greatly delight the individual. To dream that you kiss a bride shows a reunion between lovers.

Bridge

To dream that you're crossing a dangerous bridge, even though you've been advised against doing so, and you cross over it without a problem, denotes good business, and that you will achieve success quickly. To dream of crossing a railroad bridge with a speeding train coming toward you, and you are forced to jump down and hang on under the bridge by your hands in order to save yourself, indicates success and rewarded efforts in business.

Briers

To dream of being pricked by briers shows that you are disregarding good advice. This dream signifies a need to look to properties and adhere to them.

Brooms

To dream of brooms is a good sign; it tells of rapid strides towards success.

Broth

To dream of eating or serving broth suggests that success will come if you take a simple, basic approach to what you are striving for.

Brothel

To dream that you frequent a brothel indicates that your reputation is at stake through your material indulgences.

Brothers and Sisters (Alive)

To dream of siblings who are alive implies that their qualities are useful to you in your life, if you will incorporate them.

Brothers and Sisters (Deceased)

To dream that you see your deceased brothers or sisters signifies a blessing from them and good fortune about to cross your path.

Brush

To dream of using a brush of any description foretells that a mixed line of work will be assigned to you, yet you will find pleasure and reward in doing it.

Buffalo

To dream of buffalo is a sign of launching an enterprise in which you will persevere and gain large profits.

Bugle

To dream you hear a bugle playing suggests sad news about to arrive.

Bugs

To dream of seeing bugs crawling out of your toilet articles denotes an imminent illness to the dreamer. To dream that you crush a bug with your fingers signifies that you will get a letter from a blood relative telling you of a financial emergency and requesting your aid financially. To dream that your head is literally covered with bugs, and that they are inserting their heads into your scalp, denotes a disappointment pertaining to honor.

Building

To dream that you are building something signifies that you

will shortly meet with honor and distinction. To dream that you see a large building denotes that you will shortly meet a new acquaintance and will afterwards become intimate. To a lady, this dream means a new admirer.

Bull

To see a bull follow you tells of trouble in business. To see one horning a person means bad luck may overtake you.

Burglars

To dream that burglars are rifling your pockets denotes that you will have enemies to contend with. To see your home or place of business ransacked by burglars is a sign that your good name will be attacked. Here, your courage should defend you.

Buried Alive

To dream you are buried alive warns that you are spending too much time in career matters and ignoring other important aspects of life.

Burn

To dream that you are burning yourself is a good sign; it denotes that your ambition will be achieved and that you will enjoy good health.

Business

To dream that you are going into business, but are disappointed in the quality of the merchandise you receive, denotes disappointment in a letter containing important news. To dream that you have been unable to find a suitable location for the business you intend to open, or that you return inventory already paid for only to learn the shipment has been destroyed in transit, signifies a loss of personal property. To dream someone is trying to put you out of business denotes that you have been cheated in some purchase.

Butcher

To dream of a butcher cutting up a carcass indicates something will fall apart, but will still have a good outcome afterwards. To see yourself butchering in a way that is unpleasant to you signifies a need to ease up on something, lest you overdo it.

Butter

To dream that you are eating fresh butter denotes that your plans will be carried out successfully and that you will be richly rewarded. To eat rancid butter speaks of many struggles relating to manual labor.

Butterfly

To dream of a butterfly is a sign of happiness, success, and much popularity.

Buttons

For a young woman to dream that she is sewing on buttons denotes that soon she will meet a wealthy man who will become her partner in marriage. To a youth, this signifies honor and wealth.

Buy

To dream of buying things that are useful to you is a good omen of success in your endeavors. To dream of buying objects that turn out to be useless is a warning to make an upcoming decision carefully, lest you make the wrong choice.

C

"And yet, as angels in some brighter dreams
  Call to the soul when man doth sleep,
So some strange thoughts transcend our wonted themes,
  And into glory peep."

HENRY VAUGHN, British poet

Cab

To dream you are being driven in a cab denotes that you will receive the help you need. To drive someone in a cab means you will have the opportunity to help another.

Cabbage

To dream of cabbage is, as a rule, not good; it indicates trouble in many forms. Should you see green cabbage it would mean troubles in love and unfaithfulness in marriage. To dream that you are gathering cabbage denotes that your extravagance might bring you poverty.

Cabin

To dream of living in a cabin signals a need to simplify your life. To see a cabin that you would like to live in implies a need to rethink your values.

Cable Car

To see a cable car hints that you are using outdated methods to try to achieve something.

Cage

To dream of a cage with a bird inside implies that much wealth and many splendid things are coming your way. It is also a sign of a wealthy marriage. To dream of a cage that has animals inside, if the animals appear tame and peaceful, means that you will triumph over your enemies.

Cake

To dream of baking a cake signifies celebration and joy. To eat cake hints at sharing in someone else's joy. However, if the cake is eaten too quickly, or its ingredients turn foul, this suggests you are partaking of too many rich, sweet foods. To dream of cakes is usually a favorable omen. Large and luscious-looking cakes denote much success in some new enterprise; you will also receive much pleasure from both society and business.

Cakewalk

To dream that you are dancing the cakewalk, or performing cakewalk movements, implies that you will receive news from an old friend regarding other acquaintances.

Calf

To dream of a newborn calf is a signal that something new in your life requires gentle care. To dream of a peaceful calf grazing on the hills foretells of much joy and many pleasant associates, and is a sign of early good fortune.

Camel

To have a dream of a camel foretells a fortunate, long-term investment.

Camera

To dream of a camera signifies that changes may bring about unpleasant results. To dream you are taking pictures denotes that something will occur that will be very displeasing to you.

Canary Birds

To dream of these singers indicates unexpected joy. To dream that you own a canary bird foretells that you will acquire much honor and distinction.

Candles

To dream of one burning candle suggests that by taking time to be quiet and reflect within, you will resolve a problem. To dream that you see many candles burning denotes that a nice little fortune will be yours someday. To a woman, this tells that a splendid offer of marriage is approaching her, which she should not hesitate to accept. To dream of many candles burning at a church altar is a signal that prayer and giving assistance to another will bring spiritual advancement.

Candy

To dream that you are eating candy that is pleasing to your

taste denotes that you will have some money refunded that has already been paid.

Cane (Stick)

To dream you lean on a cane or a stick suggests that you will need help with something and will find it. If you dream of throwing away the cane or stick, it indicates more independence and freedom will soon be attained.

Cane (Sugar)

To dream that you see a field of cane is a good sign. It foretells advancement in your business in the near future and is a strong indication that prosperity lies ahead.

Cannon

To hear a cannon boom is a sign of something that falls through. To see a cannon ready to be fired indicates a precarious situation, but one that may still be salvaged.

Canoe

To dream that you are canoeing on a perfectly calm stream tells that you believe in your abilities and are a born leader; consequently, you should seek a venture on your own. To dream that you are on rough water means much trouble in the beginning of any business venture.

Cap

To dream of seeing a cap relates to some public work, perhaps to take part in some festivity. To dream of losing a cap means that your courage will fail you in time of danger, and that you should be cautious.

Cards

To dream of playing a card game, such as poker or blackjack, warns you not to take unnecessary chances in the coming period. To dream of playing card games that are not based on chance signifies an increase in pleasant social activities.

Carpenter

To dream that you see carpenters at work denotes success for you, acquired in a legitimate way, with little danger of losing your investment.

Carpet

To dream of a clean carpet that is a pleasant color denotes much wealth and many true friends. To dream that you are laying carpet means you will have cause to go on a pleasant journey—also a profitable one.

Carriage

To dream of riding in a horse-drawn carriage implies that you need not rush in this period of your life, but may proceed at a leisurely pace. To see a carriage standing idle implies that you are taking too slow a pace with your responsibilities.

Carrots

To dream of carrots foretells happiness in a romantic relationship, or is an omen that strength and luck are with you.

Carrying

To dream you are carrying another person indicates that you can assist someone who will soon need your help. To dream that you are carried by another signifies that you will seek another's help and receive it.

Cars

To dream of cars always refers to journeys and many changes. To dream that you have missed a ride by car and are upset over it denotes that you will be prevented in promoting your business.

Carving

To dream that you are carving a roast or a fowl is not an omen of great worldly success, as others may constantly hamper you in your efforts. To dream of carving meat of any kind, and if your present business is poor, it would be advisable to change or conceive new methods to improve your present condition.

Cash

To dream that you have an abundance of cash, but which is not yours, denotes that your friends think you are greedy and unfeeling. To dream that you spend borrowed money tells that your motives will be discovered in your deceptive generosity and that others will be offended.

Casket

To dream that you see a casket and remove the lid denotes that you will adorn the casket of a relative with flowers.

Castor Oil

To dream of castor oil denotes that you are accusing a friend based on the hearsay of another, which is unjust.

Cat

To dream that a vicious cat attacks you and you are unable to chase it away foretells that you have desperate enemies who will blacken your reputation and cause the loss of property through fire, from which legal difficulties may arise. If you are able to scare the cat away, you will overcome great obstacles. To dream of a cat that appears tame and gentle speaks of deceptive friends who may not injure or harm you bodily, but who annoy you by gossiping about you personally.

Caterpillar

To dream of a caterpillar denotes a tendency to be placed into embarrassing situations, and little chance for progress. It also speaks of deceptive friends. You would do well in being cautious with whom you speak.

Cathedral

To dream of being in a cathedral indicates great spiritual strength and a search for spiritual meaning in life. It is an omen of providential assistance.

Cattle

To dream of fat cattle shows the beginning of a successful period in your life. To dream of lean cattle suggests that you use resources wisely, as you are entering a period of scarcity.

Cave

To dream you are in a cave suggests emotions and hidden thoughts that need to be explored. To leave a cave and come into the sunlight again denotes that you are in the process of emotional recovery.

Celery

To dream of celery is a favorable omen. It speaks of prosperity and power beyond your wildest hopes. To eat celery means that unlimited love and affection will be showered upon you.

Cellar

To dream of a cellar is often a sign of approaching illness. It is also a sign that you may lose confidence in your business associate, and thereby lose property. For a young woman to dream of a cellar denotes an offer of marriage from a gambler.

Cemetery

To dream of a neatly arranged and well maintained cemetery denotes that you will enjoy prosperity. It is also a sign that you will regain property that you had figured as lost, or perhaps that you will hear of friends or relatives that you have mourned as dead.

Cesspool

To dream that a sink or cesspool is overflowing and its contents go in all directions denotes that stormy elements may destroy personal property.

Chains

To dream of breaking a chain denotes torment and difficulties. To see another bound in chains means a loss of money or an unpleasant business engagement.

Chair

To dream of a chair indicates that you will fail to keep some important obligation. To see another sitting in a chair speaks of some bad news.

Chalk

To see an unused piece of chalk near an empty blackboard denotes teaching ability. To see yourself writing on a blackboard with chalk signifies a new position of authority.

Champagne

To dream of merrily drinking champagne suggests achievement. To see others drink champagne in a dream implies that you will be passed by in some assessment.

Chariot

To dream of driving a chariot is a signal that you need to take control of an area of your life that is not working well.

Charity

To see someone doing an act of charity in a dream is a reminder not to neglect good deeds toward others. If an act of charity is done to you, it means you will be forgiven for a past transgression.

Cheated

To dream that someone has cheated you in a deal denotes that you will meet deceitful people who will try to steal part of your fortune. For the young to dream of being cheated tells of quarrels and troubles in love.

Checkers

To play checkers in a dream signifies a time of leisure and rest, as in childhood. If the game is at a standstill, however, it suggests you are stuck in some childish habit, and you need to end it.

Cheeks

To dream that you or someone else has fat and rosy cheeks is a sign that your attitude toward life is on the right track and will bring you opportunities and good fortune. To dream of pale, very lean, or scarred or wrinkled cheeks invites you to examine your attitude toward life, which may be creating problems for you.

Cheese

To dream of eating cheese speaks of sorrows and difficulties. To make cheese denotes profit and gain.

Cherries

To dream of picking cherries out of season denotes an annoyance from an enemy or former friend. To dream that you are eating a dried cherry and find that the pit resembles the shape of a diamond signifies that you will hear news of a bitter disappointment.

Chess

To dream of playing chess with a stranger foretells challenges to come in a career. If you win, you overcome the challenges. To dream of playing chess with an acquaintance or family member suggests that a quarrel, which features behind-the-scenes intrigue, may be imminent.

Chestnuts

To dream that you find chestnuts and eat them denotes success in love, or that you will meet with some pleasant experience with the opposite sex. To eat boiled chestnuts implies that you will have success in business. To dream you prick your hands with the burr, shows that you will be deceived by someone pretending to be a friend.

Chickens

For you to dream of a brood of chickens tells of many cares and petty worries, some of which will ultimately turn to your benefit. Young chickens are a good dream omen if you are contemplating some venture.

Children

To dream of children is a splendid omen. If a woman dreams of giving birth to a child, it denotes a legacy. If a young girl dreams of giving birth, she should exercise much care or she will lose her virtue. To dream that you see a child dropping from a boat into water, and then being rescued safely, means good news is on its way. To dream of seeing several children around the house is good, and if the dreamer in reality has none, it means success and many blessings. To dream of seeing your child ill or dead, it would be well for you to exercise much care and good judgment, as the child's welfare may be threatened. To dream of a dead child implies that troubles are imminent. To dream of playing with children denotes that much happiness is in store for you. To see a child at play in your dreams can foretell that you will be careless in your morals or pleasures, thereby breaking a loved one's heart.

Chimes

To dream of hearing or seeing chimes denotes prosperity, success in love, and beautiful children.

Chimney

To dream of a chimney on a roof is an indication of passion soon to be displayed.

China

For a woman to dream of cleaning or arranging her treasured pieces of china denotes that she will be domestic and home-loving in her views. This will help her to acquire many cherished possessions that she will truly value as she creates a loving home for her family.

Chocolate

To dream of drinking chocolate denotes that you will prosper after you have conquered your little difficulties. To see chocolate tells that you will provide considerably for those who are looking to you for support.

Christ

To dream of Christ denotes contentment and that you are greatly loved by your fellowmen, highly esteemed, and will gain much from the prestige and influence of others.

Christmas Tree

To dream of a Christmas tree tells of good fortunes and many joyful occasions.

Church

To dream of entering a church denotes benevolence and honorable conduct. To pray in one means joy and consolation. Should you enter a church in gloom, you will soon attend a funeral.

Cider

To dream that you drink cider denotes a dispute and that you are confiding in friends who are not worthy of sharing your confidences.

Cigar

For a member of a young couple to dream of a cigar foretells that a child will soon be conceived. If you smoke a cigar, you will be successful in a new endeavor. But if the cigar remains unlighted, there will be detrimental delays.

Circus

To dream of a circus coming to town suggests a period of play and relaxation when you can behave as a child again. To see lions and tigers in cages at a circus suggests you have strong emotions that need to be held in check. If a high-wire act is observed and successfully carried out, you will encounter something risky that will cause tension and fear, but you will survive the ordeal.

Cistern

To dream that you fall into a cistern denotes troubles caused by trespassing on the rights and pleasures of others.

City

To dream that you are in a strange city, or are lost in a city, denotes that you will soon move away from home.

Clairvoyant

To dream of being clairvoyant speaks of a possibility of changing your present occupation, which may arouse much hostility with your new associates, thereby making it unpleasant for you. To dream of consulting one implies friction in your family affairs.

Clam

To dig for clams is a good omen and promises success to the thrifty. To see a single clam lying still before you is a signal to remain quiet in some matter.

Clergy

To dream of a clergyman with a serious demeanor is a signal that you may be neglecting your own spiritual life and ideals.

If the clergyman is relaxed or bestowing a blessing, it denotes that a spiritual life is on track.

Climb

To dream that you are climbing and reach the desired spot denotes honor and distinction for you.

Cloak

To see someone wrapped in a cloak is a signal not to reveal all you know to others, especially in an important matter.

Clock

To dream of a clock denotes trouble from a backbiter. To hear a clock strike means you will hear some bad news, perhaps that of an illness, or the death of a near friend.

Closet

To dream of an open closet predicts that what was hidden will now come to light. To see a dark closet indicates hidden aspects of your feelings or actions that may create unhappiness. To see a closet being cleaned out predicts a change for the better in your home life.

Clothes

To dream of seeing old and soiled clothing denotes that a conspiracy is under way to harm you. Be cautious when dealing with friendly strangers. For a woman to dream that her clothes are soiled or torn means there is danger of someone maligning her character. To dream of clean and new clothes is an excellent omen. To dream that you have a very large wardrobe, in fact, so many clothes that you don't know what to do with them all, is a sign that you may encounter financial hardships. Sometimes legal difficulties are threatened.

Clouds

To dream that a cloud canopy is hanging over the earth implies that bad luck is due. Should clouds turn into rain, this denotes troubles caused by sickness. To dream that you see bright clouds denotes that happiness will be yours.

Clover

To dream of a single four-leaf clover indicates a lucky twist of fate that will be yours. To dream of a field of clover is very lucky, predicting a period when all will go your way.

Cloves

To dream of cloves suggests a matter or a person that gets your attention. It will be something new and beneficial.

Clown

To dream of seeing a clown performing denotes annoyances from near associates.

Clubfoot

To see someone with a clubfoot denotes suffering ahead and the need to swallow your pride in order to survive.

Coach

To dream that you are driving a horse-drawn coach full of

people signifies that you will be surprised by a meeting or a visit from a friend or relative.

Coal Mine

To dream of being in a coal mine signifies hard labor that brings little in return for a while. You are advised to bear this period with patience, for though it seems long, it will pass.

Coals

To dream of seeing red-hot coals denotes a change and many pleasures.

Coast

An ocean coast that is rocky and rough indicates strong emotional reactions to a difficult situation soon to come. A sandy and peaceful coastline signifies support from others and a time of peace.

Coat

To dream of a warm and good-looking coat foretells happiness and a long life. A tattered coat that is not warm enough is a signal that your prosperity is in danger.

Cobbler

To dream of a cobbler or shoemaker hard at work implies that what created difficulties in the past will no longer trip your path. To see an idle shoemaker implies that what you neglect could serve to make your future path difficult.

Cock Crowing

To dream that you hear a cock crowing in the early morning is a good omen. For a single person, it foretells an early marriage and all the comforts of home. To dream of seeing cocks fight foretells disaster in your family affairs that may lead to separation.

Cockroach

To see a number of cockroaches warns of unforeseen nuisances that are building up and will appear to manifest suddenly. To see a single cockroach denotes a problem that will be difficult to get rid of.

Cocktail

To dream that you are drinking cocktails denotes that you will have troubles with your friends through a fault of yours, perhaps through jealousy that you may arouse by not treating them equally.

Coffee

To dream that you are drinking coffee, if you are single, is a sign that you will have oppositions regarding marriage. If married, dreaming of coffee means possible family trouble that can be avoided by proper care.

Coffin

To dream of a coffin is an unfavorable omen. It means unavoidable losses to a man in business. To dream of seeing your coffin means much unpleasantness from the opposite sex.

Coins

To dream of gold coins indicates much success; consequently, you may be traveling extensively. To dream of silver coins is not so fortunate; they usually bring about strife and contention in the dreamer's life.

College

To see a college or university setting in a dream denotes you have made strides in understanding life and yourself. If you have inclinations toward more studies, it is an encouragement.

Comb

To dream of a comb is a signal that your thinking needs to be sorted out.

Comedy

For you to act in a comedy in your dreams is a sign that you will waste time by indulging in short-lived pleasures.

Comets

To dream you see a comet or a star with a streaming tail signifies a sudden opportunity or creative idea that comes to you unexpectedly.

Comfort

To dream that you are being comforted foretells sad news regarding a loved one, or it signifies an unfortunate outcome for a project, but because you are comforted, it foretells that eventually you will triumph.

Command

To dream of watching someone command in an overbearing manner signifies problems with authority that you are forewarned to sidestep. To dream that you are commanding others gracefully denotes that your position in life will advance in the near future.

Companion

To dream of seeing an old companion may bring about anxieties and perhaps temporary illness.

Compass

To see a compass pointing north hints that you should trust your own judgment in upcoming decisions. If the compass wavers, it suggests you need more information before making a decision.

Complexion

To dream of a clear, glowing, healthy complexion shows that you are very much on track in life and are heading toward success. To dream of a scarred complexion signifies that past hurts continue to hold you back from attaining success. To dream of pimples on your face suggests that your own angry and negative attitudes are causing you harm, and need to be cleared up.

Composing

To dream that you are engaged in composing denotes that some hard-to-solve difficulties will arise.

Conceit

To dream someone is conceited suggests a strong character.

Concert

To attend a concert signifies that much of interest will soon enter your life, and you will enjoy it.

Concubine

For a man to dream of being with a concubine is an indication that he is in great danger of public disgrace; his dual life will be brought to light. For a woman to dream that she is a concubine denotes that she has little self-respect and does not care about public opinion.

Confession

To dream of making a confession to anyone denotes a need to communicate inner feelings that have been held back. Doing so will free you and propel your life in a new direction.

Confidence

To see someone exuding confidence in a dream suggests you should concentrate on building up your own confidence.

Conservatory

To dream of being in a conservatory of music foretells your happiness and success.

Conspiracy

To dream of entering into a conspiracy suggests the need to communicate discreetly in order to accomplish something.

Constipation

If you are constipated in a dream, it suggests you are refusing to express your feelings towards others, especially with feelings of love. Unexpressed anger may be the cause of your withholding.

Contract

To dream of signing a contract, and feeling good about it, is encouragement toward business dealings and making a commitment. To see an unsigned contract warns that an agreement you are asked to enter into is better left alone.

Convent

To see a convent at a distance suggests ideals that have been forgotten should be thought about and used. For a woman to be inside a convent indicates touching her own spirituality, and is an encouragement.

Convict

To see a convict suggests you will be coerced into doing something you do not like. To be a convict in a dream is a signal to accept circumstances as they are, since change is not presently in your control.

Cooking

To dream that you are cooking implies that you will be asked to perform some pleasant duties. Friends will visit whom you thought had no regard for you. You have creative talents that need to be used. If you cook a specific food, such as vegetables, it indicates that your system needs more of that type of food to ensure continued good health.

Copper
To see copper signifies unusual gifts and items that will cross your path. To see copper pipes or fittings in a home denotes a sound foundation and a secure life.

Copying
To dream that you are copying indicates an unsuccessful plan which you thought would succeed.

Corn
To dream of corn is a good omen; it speaks of many pleasures and a successful career. To dream that you helped to gather a large heap of corn is an indication that you will rejoice in the prosperity of some friend.

Corns
To dream that your corns are painful denotes that enemies are trying to injure you. Should you dream that you succeeded in getting rid of your corns, it indicates that you may inherit a legacy from some unknown source.

Corpse
To dream that you see a corpse lying in a coffin foretells that you will receive sad news, perhaps the illness of a friend, usually the opposite sex. To dream of many corpses lying in state, yet with nothing distressing about them, is an omen of great

success and, in some cases, portends an apology from one who has deeply wronged you in the past.

Corset

To dream that you have much difficulty in removing your corset indicates that you will have an argument with a friend upon the slightest cause.

Cotton

To wear cotton is an invitation to live life in a more natural way. To see fields of cotton growing denotes benefits arising from that which comes easily and naturally to you.

Couch

To dream of lounging on a couch denotes that you are laboring under a false impression regarding some happening. Think twice before you speak.

Counterfeit Money

To dream of counterfeit money suggests your values and morals require some examination, lest you leave the straight-and-narrow path.

Counting

To dream of counting some objects is a good omen. It denotes financial stability and that you are perfectly able to meet your obligations. Should you dream of counting money, it is a sign of losses. To count to yourself is good; to count out loud is bad.

Country

If city people dream of being in the countryside, it suggests that a change of scene and relaxation will do them good. If country folk dream of the country, it indicates an expansion of business and career opportunities.

Cousin

To spend time with a cousin in a dream denotes benefit from a close friend.

Coward

To dream of a coward is a signal to take courage in hand and press forward toward your goals.

Cowboy

To see yourself as a cowboy in a dream indicates a desire for freedom. You are advised to find more self-expression in life.

Cows

To dream of cows is a good omen; it foretells an abundance of food throughout life.

Crabs

To dream of seeing crabs crawl denotes that you will be compelled to solve many complicated affairs. The dreamer, if single, may have rivals in love affairs.

Cracker

To see or to eat a small, thin cracker hints that something you are considering will not amount to much. Or, it may indicate that something needs to be cracked or opened up, before it can proceed.

Cranes

To dream of these elegant and exotic birds denotes unusual people will soon enter your life, and bring much that is new and entertaining.

Cream

To dream of cream in any form or quality is an excellent omen. It denotes that you will be associated with riches and have a bright future before you.

Cricket

To dream that you hear the noise of a cricket is an unpleasant indication of serious news, perhaps death.

Criminal

To dream that you see the escape of a criminal who has committed a crime denotes that you will be annoyed by friends who desire your influence for their own personal gain. To dream of apprehending a criminal foretells that you will come into the possession of secrets that may jeopardize your freedom.

Cripple

To see an unfortunate cripple in your dream denotes that you will be asked for charity by an old associate. It would be safe for you to give a helping hand, because someday you will be rewarded for your kindness.

Crocodile

To dream of a crocodile is a signal that someone has harmful or negative intentions toward you. You should examine new associations, and protect yourself more than usual for a period of time.

Crops

To dream of fields of wheat, or other grains growing in a lovely landscape, predicts a time of prosperity and savoring the fruits of your labors. It suggests you will have as much work as you want, in an idyllic setting.

Cross

To dream of a cross implies that there is immediate trouble ahead, so prepare for difficulties.

Crow

To see crows in your dream indicates unpleasant news. To hear them caw means that others may influence you against your better judgment in some business proposition.

Crown

To dream of a crown or of wearing a crown is an indication that you are about to excel at something, or win a competition. It thus portends honor and glory.

Crutches

To dream that you are compelled to use crutches denotes that you are too dependent and lack self-reliance.

Crying

To dream that some dear friend comes to you crying and is seemingly in deep trouble denotes that you will learn of some loss, either by fire or water, in which you may not be interested financially, but would be from a sympathetic standpoint. To a working individual, this dream may denote a loss of position. To dream that you are crying denotes that some happy affair will settle into gloom. To see others crying implies that you will hear about the financial troubles of some near relative, which is pitiful.

Cucumbers

To dream of eating cucumbers denotes vain hopes; but to the sick, it denotes recovery.

Cup

To dream of a full cup signifies good tidings and a full career. An empty and unwashed cup implies that you need to revise career directions and apply yourself more diligently in order to achieve success.

Cut

To dream of a cut denotes a possible illness, or that supposed friends' reprehensible conduct may disturb your cheerfulness.

D

"And dreams in their development have breath,
And tears, and tortures, and the touch of joy;
They leave a weight upon our waking thoughts,
They take a weight from off our waking toils,
They do divide our being… "

LORD GEORGE GORDON BYRON, English poet

Daffodils

To dream of these spring flowers foretells an end of troubles. If a person has been single, they signify an upcoming relationship filled with love. If a career has been blocked, the dream predicts opportunities that will lead to success.

Dagger

To see a dagger in you dream denotes enemies. If you succeed in getting it away from your attacker, you will conquer your enemies.

Dairy

To dream of being in a dairy and watching cows being milked denotes the need to cooperate with others in order to achieve something.

Daisy

To dream of this flower suggests innocence and a desire for simplicity.

Dance

To dream of attending a dance signifies a joyful, upcoming interaction. To dance with someone special is a sign of success in any enterprise.

Dancing

To dream of dancing signifies much pleasure and a possible inheritance.

Dandelion

To dream of dandelions implies health, happiness, and success in your future.

Dandruff

To dream that your hair is full of dandruff indicates outdated attitudes and actions that you need to let go of.

Danger

To dream you shun danger is a warning to tread carefully in your reactions to others. If a vehicle such as a car is involved, it is a warning to be cautious while driving for a period of time. To be faced with a danger that you overcome indicates a challenge that you face; but you will triumph over it.

Darkness

To dream that it becomes dark while you are traveling generally means a lack of success in something you are about to attempt.

Dates (Fruit)

Eating dates suggests a busy period is soon to come.

Dates (Social)

To dream of going on a date suggests a need for more formal social interactions and more evenings out.

Dead

To dream of speaking to a dead relative or friend is a reassurance that they are well, and it is a reminder to cherish the good they represented.

Deafness

To dream of a deaf person implies that you are ignoring something important in your life that others are suggesting. You are advised to listen carefully, which will bring success. To dream you are deaf, while in reality you are not, is a sign you will lose money in a bad investment unless you exercise great care. If you are not involved in business dealings, it implies that listening carefully to others will further your standing in life.

Death

To see someone dying in great pain means that you will shed

tears before the day is over, out of pure sympathy for someone who is suffering.

Debate

To engage in debate suggests that you must hash out some problem with others in order to resolve it.

Debauchery

To see yourself or others participate in debauchery is a bad omen. It suggest friends or new acquaintances could lead you away from that which you truly seek.

Debt

To dream that you have a debt, and are unable to meet your obligations, foretells worry in business or love.

Deception

To dream of being deceptive or sneaky in a dream signifies either that you are considering such actions, and are advised to avoid them; or, it hints that others are contemplating taking advantage of you in a backhanded manner, and you should keep a careful watch.

Deed

To dream of signing a deed amid happy feelings denotes a fine acquisition. If the one who signs it displays displeasure or suspicion, this is a warning of some acquisition that will be disappointing.

Deer

To dream of this animal is a good omen. To the unmarried, it speaks of deep and sincere friendship. To the married, much happiness. To kill a deer means that you will be slandered by those jealous of you.

Dentist

To dream that you are having dental work done is a sign that a supposed friend is not worthy of your confidence.

Deposed

To dream that you are deposed from a position of power or honor is a bad omen. It suggests that you should reassess your position and protect it from being undermined.

Deposit

To dream of depositing money in a bank suggests your fine values will bring you a life of success, good will, and happiness. To withdraw money denotes unexpected demands that you will need to meet.

Descend

To dream of going down a steep slope or road indicates a path in life that will soon become easier. To climb a steep hill or slope suggests that many obstacles are yet to be met before success is yours.

Desert

To dream that you are wandering through arid land denotes loss of property and, possibly, life.

Desk

To dream of writing or studying at a desk suggests that you will benefit by learning or pursuing something new, but that it will take time to absorb and implement it.

Destruction

To dream that the tools of your trade are destroyed means that you will lose business.

Detained

To dream that you are detained by one in authority indicates that something you have carried out will need to be redone and will cause problems. If the person in authority becomes friendly, it signifies that the problems will be overcome. During the period following such a dream, you are warned to follow the letter of the law in all dealings.

Detective

To dream that a detective has a charge against you, of which you are innocent, implies that success is drawing nearer to you each day. To dream that you are guilty denotes that you will lose your reputation and that friends will turn against you.

Devil

To dream of the devil is never a good omen. It speaks of bad influences working against you, deceitful friends, etc.

Diamonds

To dream that you are wearing diamonds is a sign that you

will be deceived in love, or that your lover is unfaithful. For a man to dream of this precious stone, or that he is dealing in them, is a sure sign that he will become rich and gain high position in life. To dream of diamonds means good luck, unless you dream that you have stolen them.

Diarrhea

To dream you are thus afflicted implies you are sharing your emotions too freely with others. Some reserve is advised.

Diary

To dream of keeping a diary suggests that it will benefit you to keep track of what is precious to you in some form of permanent record or display, such as a photograph collection.

Dice

To dream that you have won at dice is a sign that some kind of inheritance or unexpected money will come to you.

Digging

To dream of digging into the earth implies that you will never starve, but you will have to work very hard for what you obtain. Should you dream of finding some precious metal while digging, this means a favorable turn in your fortune. Should the ground slide back into the hole, or the hole become filled with water, this means that in spite of the most strenuous efforts, things will not come your way.

Dinner

To see yourself partaking gladly of this meal suggests that

you are nearing the end of a major task or undertaking, and it will fare well.

Dirt

To dream that something is very dirty warns of health problems. If something is only mildly dirty, it suggests that an area of your life is taking a turn for the worse, but if it is examined and a new course chosen, it can be corrected.

Discovery

To dream you make a discovery is a wonderful omen. It foretells a new creative idea, a solution to a problem, or a new venture that will be beneficial.

Disease

To dream that you have contracted venereal disease denotes misinformation from an enemy who is trying to attack your reputation to a near friend. To dream of diseases in general denotes luck and success.

Disguise

To dream of wearing a disguise denotes not being in touch with your true self. To see a disguise suggests you are feeling overwhelmed by another, and it is a warning to take a stand.

Dishes

To dream of breaking dishes is a signal of something being unsuitable. To see fine china in a dream foretells success and renown.

Dishonesty

To dream of dishonesty warns you not to be dishonest, lest you suffer the consequences. But if you are honest in all endeavors, it warns that someone else will try to deceive you.

Ditch

To dream of falling into a ditch signifies that you should beware of accidents for a period of time, and warns you to be sure that property and material goods are sufficiently protected.

Diving

To dream of diving into clear water denotes a favorable end to some unpleasant ordeal. If the water is muddy, things will go from bad to worse.

Divorce

To dream of divorce is a sign that you are not happy with your companion, and that the two of you should try to steady one another and avoid finding faults, or the marriage will fail.

Doctor

To dream of a doctor is a good omen, denoting prosperity and good health, particularly if one visits socially; for you will then not have to spend your money for services rendered. To dream that you send for a doctor because you are ill may indicate some friction in the family. To dream of surgery, but no blood is seen, denotes that you will be annoyed by some person who tries to blackmail you. For a girl to dream of a doctor implies that she is foolishly thinking of things which may cause trouble for her. To dream that she is sick, and has the doctor, denotes that sorrow is in store for her. For a married woman to dream of a physician denotes that she lacks self-control and imagines illness which does not exist.

Dogs

To dream of a vicious dog, yet you succeed in keeping him away, implies that you will conquer your enemies. To dream that a dog is giving birth means an irritating disappointment will work out to your advantage in the end. To dream of dogs is, as a rule, good; but if the dog snarls or barks at you, it means quarrels relating to business, and that jealous enemies want to destroy your reputation.

Dolphin

To dream of a dolphin in the water hints that you will find assistance needed for something. To dream of following a dolphin or a school of dolphins is a signal that you should take advice from an acquaintance regarding the future.

Doves

To dream of doves denotes happiness and peace, and that harmony will reign supreme in your family. It is a sign that you will be blessed with happy and obedient children.

Dragon

To dream of confronting a dragon means that the struggle for success is yet to come. To dream of slaying a dragon foretells a hard-won victory in career, health, or love, whichever area of life has hitherto not been successful.

Drama

To dream that you witness a drama relates to pleasant meetings with some distant friends. Should the drama fail to be interesting to you, it means that you will be forced to associate with unpleasant companions.

Dress

To dream that you find a woman's dress, or to dream that someone else is wearing apparel in your wardrobe, signifies troubles and irritations caused by a woman. The trouble will usually occur at a very delicate moment that proves to be very annoying.

Drinking

To dream that you're going into a public place for a drink and see acquaintances whom you invite to join you, if you are having a fun evening, means that you will make an investment or begin a new business. Should a relative refuse your invitation to join you for a drink, this means that you will meet an old acquaintance and have a long chat.

Driving

To dream that you are out driving with family or relatives, and you come across unpleasant roads, denotes a pending unfortunate occurrence. For a man to dream that he is driving with a woman is a sure sign of disappointment; for a woman to dream she is driving with a man foretells a gain or success in business.

Drowning

To dream that you see another drowning, or that you are drowning yourself, denotes much good luck for the dreamer; to a lover, an early marriage. To a girl, it will be well for her to keep an eye on her sweetheart.

Drugstore

To see a drugstore in a dream implies an upcoming illness. If you get a prescription filled, or the dream ends on a positive note, the illness will be a short one and you will recover. If the medicine is not found or the dream ends on an unhappy note, it is a more serious ailment.

Drummer

To see someone drumming in a pleasant manner denotes that satisfying work will cross your path. If the drumming is dire and distressful, you will have cause to grieve and feel sorrow.

Ducks

To dream of these fowls denotes a surprise by a friend who may call and dine with you. To see them killed speaks of enemies who may interfere with your activities. To see them flying foretells a change in business for the better. To hunt them means a possible difficulty with your employer.

Dust

To dream that you are covered with dust is a sign that you may have some losses in business through the failure of others.

This would hold true particularly if it should rain on you while you are covered with dust.

Dyeing

To dream that you are dyeing fabric is a sign that a disaster lies ahead, which may delay progress in your efforts, at least for the time being.

E

"Is this a dream? O! if it be a dream,
Let me sleep on, and do not wake me yet."

HENRY WADSWORTH LONGFELLOW, American poet

Eagle

To dream that you see an eagle soaring above you indicates high ambition, which you will have great difficulty in realizing; nevertheless, you will gain your desires by persevering. Should you dream of killing an eagle, it signifies that you will associate with people of high standing who will bring you an influential position and power in life. To dream that you ride on an eagle's back foretells that you will make a long journey, very likely into a foreign country.

Ear

To dream your ears are well-shaped shows you will achieve fame; but if the ears are deformed or misshapen, your reputation will be sullied. To dream of an ear that is cut off foretells of someone, either you or an acquaintance, who is behaving in a fanatical manner and needs to calm down.

Earrings

To dream of earrings is an omen that you will have encouraging and interesting work to do.

Earth

To dream of dark, black, rich soil signifies that something you are about to begin will turn out extremely well. If the earth is pale or contains vermin, it fares ill for the new venture.

Earthquake

To dream the earth is trembling or quaking signifies unexpected changes that will be disruptive. If a house caves in during the earthquake, it tells of an illness that will erupt without warning.

Earthworms

To dream of earthworms signifies that matters left in another person's hands are being handled unwisely and need your attention.

Eating

To dream that you are eating alone is an indication of losses and depressed spirits. To eat with others or in company denotes success, happy environments, and undertakings that will be profitable.

Eclipse

To dream of the sun in eclipse signifies the loss of your father;

if the moon is in eclipse, it denotes the death of your mother. However, if both parents are in good health, then an eclipse indicates sudden changes in either love or career.

Ecstasy

To feel ecstasy in a dream is a blessing. If the dream is filled with a luminous light, angels, or someone who leaves you feeling strengthened, it is a great blessing.

Editor

To dream you are an editor implies honor and respect in handling the affairs of others. Directions in communications are especially fortunate. To speak with an editor suggests that something needs revision or change that will be beneficial.

Education

To see yourself receive an education at a rudimentary level is a signal to get back to the basics in order to resolve something. If it involves higher education, this denotes fruits of your labor coming to you, due to what you have learned or are learning.

Eel

To dream of an eel that you are able to hold on to is a good omen. To see one in clear water is also a symbol of good fortune. To dream that one got away from you denotes that your business may suffer.

Eggs

To dream of an egg yolk implies that getting to the heart of a matter is important. To see someone with egg on his face means you have made a fool of yourself. To dream that you find a nest of eggs is an excellent sign; it foretells happiness and contentment. Also, it is a sign of many healthy children; to the unmarried, a happy love affair. To dream of rotten eggs speaks of troubles and losses. To dream of bird eggs, and that you crawled up a tree after them, denotes that you will gain money unexpectedly.

Election

To dream of yourself as a candidate for office foretells an opportunity to come. If you are elected, you will benefit greatly by the opportunity. If the outcome is unclear, success depends on your readiness to seize the opportunity gracefully and fulfill it.

Electricity

To dream of electricity denotes some immediate offer which will afford you much pleasure and success. Should you receive a shock, a danger may lie ahead. To see a live wire in your dream denotes that deceitful enemies are trying to overthrow your plans.

Elephant

To dream that you see an elephant is a happy omen; it tells of peace and plenty. To dream of many means you will gain fame and fortune. To feed one denotes a job change.

Elopement

To dream of such romance is unfavorable. To married people, it shows they are holding a position they are unworthy of, and may have trouble in these positions. To unmarried people, it tells of great trouble in love affairs.

Embalming

To dream of embalming denotes treachery and loss of friends. You are warned to let go of what is not working well.

Emerald

To dream of this gem signifies honor and wealth, and that you will rise above your present situation. If the emerald sparkles, happiness will soon be yours.

Employment

To dream that you are seeking employment is good; it denotes that you are very energetic and dynamic and that your services are appreciated. To dream that you have a job when you are unemployed means that you may continue to be unemployed due to lack of business.

Enemies

To dream that you meet an enemy and you attempt to apologize for some wrong committed, but the enemy ignores the apology, foretells a business disappointment. To dream that you overcome your enemies is a sign that you will succeed in your business and become rich. To conquer an enemy is a happy omen.

Engine

To dream of an engine foretells an unpleasant start of a trip, but which turns out well after you reach your destination. To dream that you see an engine wrecked indicates losses.

Engineer

To dream of an engineer denotes that which you are building in life is sound and good, and you will prosper from your labors.

Engraving

To dream that you are involved in engraving, but cannot finish the job through lack of ability, foretells a disappointment in a friend whom you are eagerly waiting to meet.

Enjoyment

To see people enjoying themselves in a dream suggests you may be working too hard and not taking the time for gaiety and socializing. If, however, the enjoyment appears superficial or overdone, it suggests you are too influenced by social pursuits and are neglecting your duties.

Entertainment

To dream that you are a guest at an entertainment where there is pleasant music denotes good news from friends who are away.

Envy

To dream of envying another suggests you should beware of

setting ambitions that are unreachable. If you see others envying you, you will succeed despite others' lack of faith; but beware of their jealousy. If the characters in the dream are unfamiliar to you, take care not to let envy of others taint your attitudes.

Escape

To dream that you escape from prison, or from a cloistered life, implies that you will have rapid rises in the business world. To dream that you make an escape attempt, and are caught in the act, speaks of unpleasant notoriety about you.

Evil Spirits

To dream of evil spirits obstructing your path or endeavors denotes a blind spot that is obstructing your path. If the spirit is befriended in the dream, you will overcome a shortcoming, and triumph.

Excrement

To dream of excrement denotes some change in your social surroundings.

Execution

To dream that you witness an execution signifies that you will suffer some loss due to others. To dream of seeing prisoners executed is a good sign; something that has been holding you back will soon be removed. Should you dream that you are to be executed, but someone will come to the rescue and save you, this denotes that you will succeed in overcoming your enemies.

Exercising

To see someone exercising or lifting weights hints that more discipline and effort will benefit you greatly in body, career, or life concerns.

Exile

To dream that you are in exile signifies lawsuits and the possibility of ending a relationship.

Eyebrows

For a woman to dream of thick, dark eyebrows suggests that she is adopting a pessimistic attitude that will attract only bad things. Should she pluck the eyebrows in the dream, it foretells that she can overcome negative attitudes and pessimism. If a man dreams of large and bushy eyebrows, it signifies that power and strength are his, which he is advised to use wisely.

Eyeglass

To dream of finding an eyeglass indicates that you have friends whom you do not care for, yet do not wish to offend by telling them so.

Eyes

To dream of seeing eyes staring at you with a hard and calculating expression warns you to be cautious of enemies who are trying to injure you. For lovers to dream of eyes denotes they will have rivals that may be victorious. To dream of losing an eye is an indication of illness. To see a wild-eyed person refers to fears that are running away with you and need to be calmed. To dream that you squint when your eyes are perfectly well denotes that there is something for you to discover that will benefit you. If the one squinting in the dream has poor eyesight, it denotes that you have been too isolated and need to interact more with others and the world in an open and warm-hearted manner.

F

"In sleep we receive confirmation—that we must go on living."

ANDREI SINYAVSKY, Russian-born French writer

Face

To dream that you see a face is a happy omen, providing it is pleasant and cheerful. A frowning face, or a distorted face, would signify trouble.

Factory

To see a factory in a dream indicates much needs to be done to achieve success in an undertaking. If the factory workers are busy, you are well on your way to achieving it. If much still needs to be set up for the factory to be in full swing, success will be long in coming. Patience is advised.

Fainting

To dream that you are fainting is a sign of possible illness; also, it can mean distressing news from distant persons. To dream of seeing others faint is a sign of good news. To see someone fainting in a dream can also suggest that you allow some circumstances to overpower you too readily; it implies a need to speak up more strongly and assert your wishes more clearly.

Fairy

To see or speak to a kindly fairy is an omen of grace that will come to you if you listen to your own inner voice. If it is a fairy or creature that is not pleasant in demeanor or communication, it signifies you are on the wrong path and out of touch with your own inner voice.

Fall

To dream that you are falling from a high place and are frightened, but receive no injuries, denotes that you will overcome a present obstacle. To suffer injuries would signify obstacles that will go from bad to worse.

Fame

To dream that you have acquired fame implies that you are following a mistaken ambition. To dream of famous people denotes that you will rise to the epitome of fame.

Family

To dream of a large family and happiness therein foretells you will help many by your benevolence and talents. If the family is not well cared for, it indicates that responsibilities will feel like burdens; nevertheless, you are advised to fulfill all duties well.

Famine

To dream of famine denotes a lack of caring for yourself or for others. You are advised to get in touch with unmet needs.

Fan

To dream of using or seeing a fan indicates that good news is waiting for you. Dreaming of a fan is also an omen of reviving an old friendship which may, in the end, prove to be very profitable and advantageous.

Farmer

To dream of yourself as a farmer is an indication of a period of hard work that lies ahead.

Farming Tools

To dream of farming tools signifies available assets that can be turned into a profit. A plow denotes an ability to bypass resistance and open up new areas in life and career. A tractor implies that the work you are engaged in will proceed slowly, but in time it will bring great rewards.

Fat

To dream that you are growing very fat tells that you will soon change from your present place, which will be good. To see others fat is also good.

Fatigue

To dream that you are fatigued denotes a run-down vitality,

which can lead to illness. In business, things will diminish in power.

Fears

To dream that you feel nervous and fearful over some matter means that your prospective plans may prove worthless. For the unmarried to dream of being frightened foretells of disappointment.

Feathers

To dream that you see feathers about you is an omen that your ambition will be achieved and that you will rise to great heights. To dream of ornamental feathers means that you will become popular.

Feces

To dream that you are discharging feces denotes a disappointment in money matters.

Feet

To dream that your feet hurt is an indication of irritations and troubles.

Fence

To dream of a long fence stretching far off into the distance denotes a long and full life. To dream of building a fence that is needed is a signal to give of time and energy to yourself and loved ones, rather than only to strangers or acquaintances. To climb over a fence signifies you will overcome something that has been holding you back. To knock down a fence predicts dealing with issues from the past.

Ferryboat

To dream of taking a ferryboat ride, and feeling a sense of lightness, suggests that something is available to help you over a difficult period or situation. If the feelings are heavy, it suggests that you will leave behind something that has been meaningful to you.

Fever

To dream you have a fever denotes that you are too worried and are wearing down your nerves needlessly. Live in the present, not in the past. Don't spoil today by worrying about yesterday. To dream of others being sick denotes that someone in the family may become ill.

Fiddle

To see a fiddle played joyfully suggests accomplishment and satisfaction. To see a fiddler playing sadly hints at unexpected sorrows. To see a fiddler play lightly, while serious events surround him, suggests you are avoiding problems.

Fight

For a businessman to dream that he is involved in a fight means he will soon make a change that will prove successful; to a non-office worker, it predicts a raise in wages. To see others fighting denotes carelessness in the spending of money and time. To dream that you defeat your assailant implies that you will win honor and wealth, in spite of any opposition toward you.

Figuring

To dream that you are adding a large column of figures, or solving a difficult problem, denotes that the dreamer must be very cautious in the presentation of a business deal, because it may fail to influence the party concerned.

Filth

To dream of filth, if you are contemplating a new home or work situation, suggests the prospect being considered will be unsavory and is best avoided. To see a part of the body in a filthy condition suggests that present habits can lead to illness or sorrow.

Fingers

To dream of fingers generally speaks of a gain. For you to dream that they are cut or hurt implies hard work throughout life. To dream that you have lost your fingers is an omen of legal difficulties over money matters.

Fire

To dream that you see something on fire, and succeed in extinguishing the blaze before it gains much headway, denotes that you will be surprised very unexpectedly. To dream of fire is a happy sign, so long as you do not get burned. To dream that your place of business is destroyed denotes that you will become very discouraged regarding your business, but some unforeseen good fortune will give you strength and renewed hope.

Firearms

To see people randomly firing guns suggests anger in you or someone around you that may be easily triggered, but does not imply physical harm. To carry a firearm, but not fire it, implies you feel threatened and need to assert yourself or change your situation.

Fire Engines

To see fire engines shining brightly at the station signifies that all is well and that what you have been anxious about is a false alarm. However, to see fire engines driving rapidly to a site suggests that something is in danger of falling apart, unless assistance is provided.

Firefly

To dream of fireflies suggests a period of relaxation in a country setting. If, however, anxiety and negativity accompany the dream, it suggests you are letting illusions and false hopes deceive you.

Fireworks

To dream of witnessing an impressive display of fireworks is a happy signal that good health and enjoyment will soon be yours, and predicts cause for celebration.

Fish

To dream of seeing fish swimming in clear water is very good; it's an omen that you will be favored by rich and powerful persons.

Fisherman

To dream that you are a fisherman suggests that you will be challenged in seeking something you desire. If you catch a fish in a dream, you will overcome the obstacles.

Fishhook

To see a dangling fishhook denotes deception to which you are vulnerable. But if the fisherman with the fishhook is happy and satisfied, it suggests that present ideas could bring fulfillment and success.

Fishing

To dream of fishing in clear water, and that you can see the fish bite and are successful in catching them, denotes that the dreamer will discover something which may be used to his advantage, resulting in wealth. If you fail to catch any fish, your efforts to obtain wealth will be difficult.

Flag

To dream of your country's flag relates to great success and victory. For the unmarried to dream of their country's flag indicates admiration from a soldier.

Flame

To see a small flame denotes a moderate situation, either in emotions or level of success. A large flame glowing brightly signifies much emotion or success. To dream of blowing on a flame so it flares higher is a warning that if you continue a certain course of action you are presently pursuing, you will stir the wrath of those around you. Putting out a flame in a dream suggests the need to calm down emotionally or to say no to something that is ardently present to you, whether in romance or in business.

Fleas

To dream of fleas indicates irritation from close associates, which may cause you to lose your temper.

Flies

To dream that you see an unlimited amount of flies about you denotes that you are in danger of being threatened with an illness; also, that enemies are trying to destroy your efforts, causing you much difficulty.

Flood

To dream that you are in clear water that floods, rises, and recedes gently denotes peace and plenty. To dream of muddy water that floods and destroys an enormous amount of property denotes sickness, troubles and losses, as well as unhappiness in family affairs.

Flowers

To see many flowers in your dream denotes pleasure and profit. For a young woman to dream of receiving flowers is a sign that she will have many suitors. To dream of withered flowers indicates a disappointment. To dream of gathering and making a bouquet of flowers reveals you have unfulfilled hopes and wishes. If the bouquet is beautiful and well-received, a wish will be realized. If the bouquet withers or is rejected, the hope will not materialize. To dream of finding flowers is a signal that you are spiritually on the right path, and it indicates a blessing.

Flowers (Artificial)

To dream that you see someone making artificial flowers or bouquets signifies that you will be astonished at an exorbitant price charged by someone who usually performs some service for you.

Flying

To dream that you are flying is a very good omen, providing you fly low. It indicates a promotion in the near future that will make you very happy. To the lover, it is a sign that your sweetheart is true to you. To fly over clear water is an omen of great marital happiness.

Fog

To dream of fog signifies confusion and possible loss. It is a warning to tread carefully and take time to think things through calmly before acting.

Forest

To dream of being lost in a forest signifies profit to the poor and loss to the rich.

Fortune-teller

To dream that you are consulting a fortune-teller implies that you are undecided regarding some important matter. It would be wise to trust your instincts and your first impression.

Fountain

To dream of seeing a fountain in the sunlight speaks of pleasant trips and numerous possessions.

Fox

To dream of a sly fox is an indication of thieves annoying you; to fight with one speaks of an enemy who is crafty and subtle. To dream of a tame fox is good; it denotes that your affections will not be betrayed.

Friends

To dream of friends being well and prosperous denotes that you may soon see them and have an enjoyable time.

Frogs

To dream of seeing frogs leap around denotes that you will have many sincere friends as your associates. To dream of catching them is often a sign of run-down vitality.

Fruits

To dream of fruit out of season denotes struggles and unpleasant things to contend with; in season, it is always good. If the fruit is ripe, it is an excellent sign of good fortune to come to the dreamer. To dream of fruit which is at its peak indicates your labors will yield success. To dream of fruit which is damaged warns that some activity or relationship needs attention, lest you lose it. To see rotten fruit, suggests something is beyond repair and it is best that you let it go.

Funeral

To dream of the funeral of a relative or friend indicates riches, happiness, legacies, and a brilliant marriage. To dream of the funeral of a stranger denotes scandal and deep underhanded practices.

Fur

To dream of a beautiful fur denotes a special favor or gift soon to come, but you must take care that it comes in honest circumstances. If the fur is old or tattered, it implies that a love that once burned bright is dying.

Furniture

To see beautiful furniture is a good omen, either of accomplishment or of attaining long-cherished goals. If the furniture is broken or ugly, you are warned to examine the state of your health or family situation, for it may speak of illness or divorce.

G

"Even sleepers are workers and collaborators in what goes on in the universe."

HERACLITUS, Greek philosopher

Gallows

To dream of seeing someone executed on the gallows implies that extreme caution must be taken to avoid pending danger. To dream that you are hanging yourself on the gallows indicates that friends are trying to malign you.

Gambling

To dream that you are gambling and win a great amount of money denotes a loss of friends. Winning can also suggest a risk is worth taking. To lose money by gambling denotes consolation and relief from problems. On the other hand, to gamble and lose can also be a warning to avoid anything risky at this time.

Garter

To see a garter in a dream, especially a blue or pink one, foretells a romance that will lead to marriage. To see one that is bright red or black signifies a steamy affair, but not necessarily a long-term relationship.

Gas
To dream that you are overcome by gas denotes that you will have an accident due to your own carelessness.

Gate
To see yourself pass through a gate suggests new ventures that will lead to unfamiliar ground. If the person walks with assurance, you will meet all new circumstances successfully.

Geese
To dream that you see geese or hear them honking implies that you will soon rise above your present circumstances. If you dream of geese swimming in clear water, it is an excellent omen.

Gems
To dream of valuable gems denotes that a happy fate is before you, both in love and in business.

Ghosts
To dream of a deceased one's spirit, if dressed in white with a cheerful expression, denotes consolation and happiness; to see one with a revolting expression means a member of the opposite sex will flatter you in attempt to win you over. For a ghost to speak to you implies that you will be protected from those who want to harm you.

Gift

To dream that you have received a gift is a splendid omen. It denotes that you have no difficulties in meeting your bills. It is also an excellent indication of genuine feelings in affairs of the heart. To send a gift means that displeasure will come your away. For a man to dream that he receives a gift from an unmarried lady tells of friendship; from a married lady, illicit proposals.

Ginger

To see ginger added to something being cooked is a signal to take a subtle, low-key, but friendly approach to endeavors. It foretells interesting new experiences.

Gingerbread

To dream of baking gingerbread foretells special occasions in which there will be reunions with loved ones. To eat gingerbread suggests that you will receive special attention and care from unexpected sources.

Girls

To dream of seeing a lot of girls foretells encouraging prospects and many joys. For a man to dream that he is a girl is a warning for him to examine his sexual desires.

Glass

To dream that you are looking into a glass, or mirror, refers to trouble in your family. To dream that someone gives you a glass and you let it fall denotes that you will have an argument with someone close to you. To dream of breaking any drinking glass warns of losing your grip on something. It warns you to be cautious in upcoming ventures, and not to give up your responsibility or power to another at this time.

Gloomy

To dream that you feel gloomy and discouraged denotes that you will soon hear very discouraging news.

Gloves

To dream that you are wearing gloves denotes honor, pleasure, and prosperity. To dream that you lost your gloves tells that you will shortly have an argument with a loved one. To dream of wearing an old pair of gloves of which you are ashamed tells that you will be deceived and may thereby lose something of value.

Gold

To dream that you find gold is an omen of honors and riches; to spend it, sorrow and disappointment. To dream of hiding gold denotes that you will get even for something done to you. To dream that you have a gold mine denotes that you will become greedy and money-hungry.

Gossip

To dream that you have been gossiping about something you had no right to denotes that you will worry about a problem. To dream that others have been gossiping about you is good; it means that a very pleasant surprise is in store for you soon.

Grammar

To dream that you are studying a book of grammar implies that you will soon make a wise investment that will prove very profitable.

Grandparents

To see your grandfather or grandmother in a dream implies you have many people around who watch over you. If your grandfather points something out to you, it signifies that you should not forget traditional values in living your life.

Grapes

To dream that you see a cluster of grapes is a good omen. If you eat some, and they were pleasing to the taste, many pleasures and successes are in store for you; if they are sour and unpleasant to the taste, it foretells sorrow and trouble. For a young girl to dream of eating grapes is an omen that she will soon marry; to pick grapes only denotes that you will meet a stranger.

Grave

To dream of a grave is not a good omen. To look into an empty grave indicates unpleasant news, generally relating to losses. To dream of digging a grave denotes that others are trying to prevent your efforts. To see your own grave also speaks of enemies that are trying to harm you.

Grease

To dream that you have grease on your body or your clothes

signifies that plans you believed to be profitable may amount to nothing.

Groceries

To dream that you have bought a lot of fresh groceries is an excellent omen. It denotes peace and prosperity.

Grocery Store

To see a grocery store denotes success and progress. But if you are searching for items and don't find them, it means disappointment, and also that a success will be snatched from you.

Guests

To dream of unexpected guests coming to visit signifies unexpected responsibilities that will be yours. If the guests are made welcome and are grateful for the hospitality, you will benefit by accepting the responsibility graciously and carrying it out well.

Guitar

For a man to dream that he hears soft strains from a guitar denotes that seductive women will try to trap him into marriage. For a young woman to dream of hearing music from a guitar means problems in her love life. To play this instrument indicates a happy family life.

Gulls

To dream of gulls is an omen that your possessions will increase rapidly in value.

Gun

To dream of this weapon is always a bad omen. To dream of hearing the sound of a gun denotes trouble in work. To dream of shooting a gun implies a misfortune.

Gypsy

To dream of this wandering tribe denotes that your immediate future is full of uncertainties. For a woman to dream that a Gypsy is reading her palm is a sign of an early but unwise marriage. For a man to dream of consulting a Gypsy tells that he is in danger of losing some valuable belongings.

H

"Myths are public dreams, dreams are private myths."
JOSEPH CAMPBELL, American philosopher

Hail

To dream that you are caught in a hail storm denotes poor success in your prospective venture. To watch hail falling indicates trouble and sadness.

Hair

For a woman to dream that she has beautiful hair, and in reality has not, denotes carelessness of her personality; also, poor mental power through lack of development. For a man to dream that he is losing his hair denotes that he may become poor through his overly generous habits. To dream that you have hair cut close to the head denotes that your willful extravagance will cause you to regret it. For a man to dream of having hair as long as that of a woman denotes weakness of character. To dream of a bald woman denotes poverty and sickness. For an unmarried woman to dream that her hair is turning gray foretells that she will find it difficult to decide which one of her lovers to choose as a husband.

Ham

To see a large ham hints that you tend to overdo things, emotionally or otherwise. To see a small, tempting slice suggests you should display more emotion and spontaneity.

Hammer

To dream of a hammer foretells hard work but good pay. It may also signify that a strong approach is required to resolve a current problem.

Hammock

To see a hammock is a signal that you require relaxation. To lie in one hints at upcoming free time. To lie in one, but to turn over and fall, means you are relaxing too much and suggests attention to work and duties is needed.

Hand

To dream of having beautiful and well groomed hands denotes that you will rapidly rise in your career and reach distinction. To dream that they are ugly or malformed speaks of disappointments and hard times. To see blood on your hands denotes quarrels and friction in your family. To dream that your hands are tied tells of troubles in business.

Handcuffs

To dream of having your wrists handcuffed denotes that you will be greatly irritated by enemies. To succeed in releasing yourself from them denotes that you will escape the plans designed for you by your enemies.

Handkerchief

To dream of a handkerchief signifies formality could be useful.

Harbor

To see ships at anchor in a harbor denotes a successful journey. If the waters are rough, it may be that a project includes challenges; but these will be overcome.

Harem

To dream that you are the keeper of a harem implies that you are scattering your best efforts on base pleasures. For a woman to dream that she is an inmate of a harem denotes that she may resort to illegal pleasures, or enjoy the attention of married men.

Harlot

To dream of being in a harlot's company denotes an overindulgence in pleasures that may end disastrously. To dream of marrying one means many undeniable and unpleasant things to face the rest of your life.

Harness

To dream of a harness foretells of responsibility that will be a long-term commitment.

Harp

For someone with an illness to hear a harp played denotes recovery. To see a harp played or to play one in a dream indicates that what you are doing is reaping spiritual rewards.

Harvester

To see many harvesters at work denotes prosperity; to see them at rest means poor success in the near future.

Hat

To dream of wearing a soiled hat predicts damage and dishonor. To dream of wearing a new hat denotes a change of home and business, which will turn out prosperously. To lose your hat implies that you will be irritated and annoyed over some business affairs.

Hatchet

To dream of a hatchet is a warning to expect danger or death. If it is broken or rusty, you will have troubles over disobedient people.

Hate

To dream of hating someone suggests that feelings from or toward another are out of control and need to be balanced.

Hawk

To dream of a hawk foretells that you are likely to be cheated by one in whom you had the utmost confidence. To succeed in shooting one implies that by persevering you will overcome all obstacles. To shoot at a hawk and miss denotes that you have enemies who are trying to malign you and destroy your good reputation in the community.

Hay

To dream that you see hay denotes that you will be invited to a party, and that you will also assist a distinguished person. To dream that you are hauling and putting hay into your barn indicates a very substantial fortune, and that you will realize a large profit from some enterprise.

Head

To dream of seeing a head severed from the body, and fresh blood around it, speaks of very bitter disappointments. To dream of seeing yourself with more than one head denotes a sudden change for the better in your occupation. To dream of the head on a savage beast denotes that your desires run on a low plane, and are given greatly to material pleasures; in fact, they are ruled by the animal world.

Hearse

To dream of a hearse implies that an illness may enter your home in the near future; however, it may not amount to much. A hearse generally portends the death of someone near, such as a close friend.

Heart

To dream that your heart is paining you, or that you feel a smothering sensation, denotes that some oversight or stupid mistake may be the cause of a loss.

Heat

To dream of intense heat suggests quarrels are brewing. If you keep an open and calm attitude, ill effects can be avoided. But if there is a scene of happiness linked to intense heat, it suggests great passion about to unfold.

Heaven

To dream that you are climbing heavenward denotes that success may come too late in life to bring happiness. To dream that you are climbing to heaven on a ladder and reach it denotes that you will rise to great power in your present career. To fail in the attempt to climb to heaven signifies that you are likely to meet with many losses.

Hell

To dream of being in hell denotes that great temptation, which will be hard to resist, will confront you.

Herbs

To dream of herbs, especially if they have a pungent odor, indicates new interests will enter your life. If the herbs smell bitter or the plants appear in poor condition, you will lose interest in present activities due to unpleasant circumstances.

Hermit

To dream of a hermit denotes great misery caused by unfaithful friends. To dream that you live the life of a hermit implies that you are very reserved, self-centered, and hard to become acquainted with.

Hiding

To dream of hiding yourself suggests that you are feeling vulnerable. This can be changed by strengthening yourself or leaving the situation.

Hill

To dream that you are climbing a hill, and reach your objective point, denotes success in a new undertaking. To dream that you are going down a hill signifies that the new undertaking will not be successful.

Hippopotamus

To see a hippo in a dream relates to something unwieldy that will cross your path. It is best avoided and left alone.

Hire

To see yourself hired denotes progress in your career. To hire others signifies the need to engage others or cooperate with them in order to achieve success.

Hissing

To dream that you hear others hissing at you denotes that you will not be pleased with the actions of some newly-made acquaintance. To dream that you are hissing at another denotes that you are not truthful to yourself.

Hoe

To dream of carrying a hoe signifies work that needs to be done before something can succeed. To hoe hard ground suggests the time is not right for beginning something. To hoe rich, black earth foretells much success in a new venture.

Hogs

To dream of looking at the actions of fat hogs foretells a change in business which will prove very profitable. Lean hogs, however, foretell trouble with employees and probable difficulties in business. To hear them squealing refers to unpleasant news, sometimes death. To see a litter of them denotes that there is a great deal of good luck in store for you.

Homesick

To dream of being homesick implies that you will refuse excellent opportunities for traveling, for which you will be sorry afterwards.

Honey

To dream of seeing honey is an omen of great wealth. To dream of eating honey denotes happiness in love; to lovers, an early marriage.

Horses

To dream of horses in general is good. To dream that the horse you're riding is exhausted, or that you come to a place you cannot cross, denotes bad news relating to business. To dream that you are trying to pass by a horse, and can't because you are afraid, signifies that you will forget or lose something valuable, but will find it again. To dream that you are riding a horse is a sign that you will rise a step higher in the world; but if you are thrown off, it refers to scandal and disgrace. To dream of exchanging horses denotes that someone will deceive you in a bargain. Selling a horse foretells a loss; to buy a horse signifies that you will make money by selling property. To dream that you clean a horse that is covered with dirt foretells a coming sickness. To dream of a wounded horse tells of news of friends who are in trouble. To dream of hearing a horse neigh is a signal of strong appetites that can become carried away; you are advised to practice moderation.

Horse Race

To dream of watching a horse race foretells competition that must be met in order to succeed. To place a bet on a horse and lose warns you not to get involved in something that appears enticing.

Horseshoe

To dream of seeing a horseshoe is an omen of luck in business; to find one denotes that your interests will advance beyond your wildest expectations. To dream of playing horseshoes predicts a happy family life.

Hospital

To dream that you are a patient in a hospital is a sign of impending disease. To dream that you are visiting a friend there denotes that you will hear bad news.

Hotel

To dream of seeing a fine hotel denotes riches and extensive travel. To dream of owning a hotel denotes a good deal of success brought about by your own personal efforts.

Hothouse

To see beautiful blooms and plants in a hothouse suggests much success can be yours, but it will take special conditions and skills to bring it about.

House

To dream that you are going through an empty house signifies trouble. To dream of building a house is an omen that you will make a wise change.

Housekeeper

To dream of having the help of a housekeeper indicates support from unexpected sources.

Hugging

To dream that you are hugging a person whom you admire implies that you will have troubles in your love affairs and probably in business. For married people to hug others, and not their partners, indicates dishonor.

Hummingbird

To see a hummingbird denotes an unusual opportunity that will come through an unexpected acquaintance.

Hunting

To dream that you are hunting denotes that you are struggling for the unattainable. To dream that you succeed in getting what you are hunting for denotes that you will overcome your obstacles.

Hurricane

To dream that you hear the roar and frightful sounds of a hurricane denotes that you will suffer hardships in trying to avoid business failure. To dream that you look at the havoc caused by a hurricane means you will avert some business trouble by sheer good luck, or perhaps through the good advice of some good friends.

Husband

To dream that your husband is in love with another woman denotes that he will soon tire of his present surroundings and seek pleasures elsewhere. To dream that your husband is about to leave, and you don't know why, implies that there is bitterness between you, which has not yet surfaced. To dream that you are in love with another woman's husband denotes that you are not happy, and are trying to change your present life.

Hydrant

To see a fire hydrant suggests that something creating anxiety need not be a cause for alarm, because safeguards are at hand.

Hydrophobia

To dream that you suffer from the fear of water denotes that enemies are trying to prevent your plans. To dream of seeing others suffer from the fear of water implies that business conditions will be affected by a death. To dream that an animal with this condition bites you is a sign that you will be betrayed by a friend in whom you hold the utmost confidence.

Hymn

To dream of singing a hymn or psalm suggests you look inward to your spiritual self to find needed answers. If a hymn is sung by a choir, it denotes that great help is available from spiritual sources.

I

"A happy dream may shed its light upon entire waking hours, and the whole day be infected with the gloom of a dreary or sorrowful one."

WALTER JOHN DE LA MARE, English writer

Ice

To dream of seeing ice float in clear water denotes that jealous friends will try to interrupt your happiness, but will not succeed. To dream that you walk on ice denotes that you will waste much time and money on temporary joys.

Iceberg

To see just the tip of an iceberg in a dream indicates hidden trouble. To see an iceberg loom over you implies that you are surrounded by those who are unappreciative or uncaring.

Ice Cream

To see a tempting dish of ice cream, but not eat it, suggests a disappointment. If you are very fond of ice cream, it can imply that eating less would be advisable. If you are eating ice cream happily, it foretells appreciation and support for your endeavors.

Icicles

To dream of seeing icicles on trees or buildings denotes that a worry that has been distressing you will soon vanish.

Idiot

To dream of being an idiot, or acting like one, is a warning to rethink a recently made decision. Or, you should look at all the alternatives in a decision you are about to make, lest you make a foolish choice.

Idle

To dream that you are idle means you will fail to accomplish what you have begun. To see your friends in idleness denotes a request for charity.

Idolatry

To dream of worshipping an image implies serious mental trouble and bad luck in business.

Image

To see an image of yourself in a dream suggests that you need to take more time to reflect on life and the course your life is taking. To see yourself as a statue suggests embarking upon a path that is inflexible, and portends that its outcome will have long-lasting consequences.

Imprison

To see yourself imprisoned tells of an unhappy burden or work situation, which, nevertheless, needs to be endured. Although it will not change quickly, the time will come when it will end. To imprison another implies you may be imposing an undue burden on another, and you should rethink it.

Imps

To dream of seeing imps is a bad omen for those who are ill, or for elderly persons. It refers to serious changes and grave hurts or disappointments to come to the dreamer in future endeavors.

Indian

To dream of a North American Indian (Native American) indicates getting in touch with nature and living in harmony with it. To dream of someone from India indicates wisdom and intuition upon which you can draw.

Indigestion

To dream of suffering from indigestion forebodes gloomy surroundings and pessimistic thoughts.

Infants

To dream of an infant is an excellent sign. It foretells happiness and joy, good luck, and general success. Lovers who dream of an infant may be sure of a happy and successful marriage. To a man in business, it foretells a successful change in business. For an unmarried woman to dream that she has an infant denotes that she will be slandered for actions she is not guilty of.

Inheritance

To dream of gaining an inheritance signifies advancement in life or career.

Injury

To dream that you have met with an injury denotes that your friends will be kind to you, and whatever is wrong will be corrected.

Ink

To dream that you are using ink is good; but to dream that you spill it denotes prolonged irritations and many spiteful things being done through envy. To dream that you have ink somewhere on your clothing or body denotes that you will cause suffering and offend someone.

Insane

To dream that you are insane forebodes a sad ending to some newly conceived project; also, that you may have to deal with illness. To see others insane indicates that your relatives or close friends may ask you for financial assistance, because they are in dire need of your help.

Inscription

To dream of writing an inscription denotes formal or legal

matters that will require your attention. You are advised to act in accordance with all requirements in present dealings.

Insult
To insult another in a dream suggests you are not in touch with how your actions or words are affecting others. To be insulted foretells some hurt coming to you spontaneously, inflicted by another.

Interpreter
To dream of interpreting anything shows an ingenious mind. Your ideas can be turned into profit.

Intestines
To dream of rupturing or suffering in your intestines denotes family arguments. To dream of seeing your own intestines denotes that you will soon suffer from sickness, which will cause you to lose time from work and, thereby, lose a paycheck.

Intoxication
To dream of being intoxicated denotes an increase of wealth and sound body. To dream that you become intoxicated by looking at liquor is a bad sign; it shows that you are trying to cover your plans by deceptive actions, which may bring you into the police court.

Introduction
To see someone introduced to another in a dream suggests

that a resolution to a problem may come through another person. It is suggested that you seek contacts and advice from others.

Invalid

To see an invalid in a dream is a signal that you are taking on an attitude that could hold you back. Keep all attitudes positive, but not naive. If the invalid is happy in the dream, you will overcome a troubling circumstance.

Invitation

To dream of receiving an invitation predicts a new talent that will unfold in you.

Iron

To dream of being injured by an iron denotes great confusion in your business. To dream that you touch a red-hot iron implies that you will have many disappointments with present plans. To see any iron suggests something that requires smoothing over or straightening out before it can proceed. To see someone ironing suggests that the process of straightening out has begun.

Island

To dream that you are on an island all by yourself, and the water is clear around you, signifies pleasant trips and profitable ventures. To dream of seeing others on an island denotes a struggle to rid yourself of unpleasant activities.

Itching

To dream that you itch all over your body tells of troubles in business, usually caused by enemies that interfere. These troubles will influence you to act in ways that are not in your best interest.

J

"In Gideon the Lord appeared to Solomon in a dream by night: and God said, Ask what I shall give thee."

1 KINGS 3:5

Jackass

To dream of a jackass is an indication that someone is acting like one, whether it be you or someone close to you. To hear one bray is a warning that stupidity may lead to loss or disappointment, but it can be averted.

Jail

To dream of seeing others in jail denotes that you will be urged to grant a favor, which you will not be happy about. For you to dream that your sweetheart is in jail denotes that you will be disappointed in his or her character. So, use caution; look into the situation before you leap.

Jam

To dream that you are eating jam that is pleasing to the taste denotes long and pleasant trips. To dream that you are making it indicates a happy home and many true friends.

Jar

To see a large jar is a signal of trouble to come. If the jar is empty, loss can occur. If the jar is full, much is at stake.

Jaws

To see the jaws of some large monster in your dreams indicates hurt feelings between you and friends. To dream that you are in the jaws of some large beast indicates that your immediate future holds many complications. To dream that your own jaw is broken implies that someone has told a vicious lie about you.

Jealousy

To dream that you are jealous of your sweetheart or life partner denotes that enemies are exerting influence over you to commit something dishonest. For a woman to dream that she is jealous of her husband denotes that her actions at home will give her husband material to make her the object of ill-timed jokes in public.

Jelly

To dream of jelly signifies sorrow and trouble and, sometimes, that the most hidden secrets shall be revealed.

Jeopardy

To dream someone is in jeopardy indicates a problem you are

attempting to solve. If the dream's ending shows tools being used or solutions being implemented, then the solution is available to you. If the dream ends unresolved, the answer is not yet at hand.

Jeweler

To see a jeweler working at this craft suggests the need to concentrate on whatever is of great interest to you, which will eventually bring much satisfaction. Or, it can signify that you will deal with items of importance, exerting an influence on the finances or minds of others.

Jewelry

To dream of jewelry denotes that much pleasure and riches will soon be yours. To dream of finding jewelry foretells getting in touch with what is important to you, which will aid you in a decision or situation.

Jewels

To dream of sparkling jewels stored in a box suggests you have many inner qualities of great value, which the world may not recognize. To be given a jewel as a gift denotes love or a special opportunity that will bring much joy. To have gems stolen foretells losing your values in a transaction that is not advisable. To steal jewels is a sign of immaturity, and of unwise ambitions and goals.

Jig

To dream of dancing a jig is an omen that you are lighthearted and gay, and love your work. To see others dancing a jig denotes that you are too easy and benevolent, and may give money which will not be used wisely.

Jockey

To see a jockey riding denotes an investment soon to come, but one that carries a risk. If the dream shows the jockey in a winning position, you can take the risk.

Jogging

To see someone jogging in a dream foretells a new endeavor that will require effort, yet bring much satisfaction. If the jogger is large in size and runs with difficulty, it suggests you are neglecting physical requirements, which could lead to health troubles later in life. If the jogger is sound of body and agile, this is an encouragement that you are living life well and should continue on the same path.

Jolly

To dream that you are feeling jolly and gay is an omen that you will have many friends that look up to you as a leader and entertainer, and will have many favors come your way.

Journey

To dream that you went on a pleasant trip denotes much success and happiness in the near future. If the trip was spoiled by accident, it foretells unhappiness and loss of hope.

Joy

To dream of joyful circumstances or festivals is an omen of a fine marriage, for one who is engaged. For one who has been beset by misfortune it is a sign of relief from a problem or a circumstance.

Judge

To dream of a judge who is overbearing suggests you are being too harsh with yourself in something you are trying to accomplish. If the judge is kindly, circumstances will turn to your advantage.

Judo

To dream of attending a judo class indicates complex learning and achievements that will be yours, and will empower you.

Jug

To dream of jugs that are full denotes that you have many true friends, and that they look out for your interests. To dream of taking a drink from a jug denotes health and strength, and that you generally look on the bright side of everything.

Jumping

To dream of jumping, and to succeed in getting where you want to be, indicates success; to fail in the attempt will bring about bitter disappointment. To dream that you are jumping over a cliff denotes a bad investment and troubles in love.

Jury

To dream that you are selected to serve on a jury implies that you are highly esteemed by your employees, and may ultimately select one to become a partner.

K

"Dreams transport us through the underside of our days."

GAIL GODWIN, American writer

Kaleidoscope

To see a kaleidoscope is a signal that change will enter your life. To look through a kaleidoscope predicts adventure and new horizons.

Kangaroo

To dream of a kangaroo signifies unexpected and unusual journeys and opportunities.

Keg

To dream of a keg denotes that your present difficulties are imaginary. Therefore, it is well not to spoil today by dwelling on what happened yesterday.

Kennel

To dream of a kennel with many dogs denotes many friendships, which need care and attention to be maintained.

Kettle

To dream of kettles denotes difficult work ahead of you. To see kettles that are boiling indicates that your struggle will soon end.

Keyboard

To see a musical keyboard in a dream implies unused talents, whether they be musical or other. If used, they will bring happiness to you and others. To see a typewriter keyboard suggests intellectual skills that can be put to use.

Keys

To dream that you lose your keys denotes things undreamed of will cross your path. To find keys is a good omen; it speaks of domestic happiness.

Kicking

To dream of kicking someone in a dream indicates unexpressed anger, or anger that was poorly expressed in the past. It implies energies that need to be redirected positively, and the acceptance of an existing situation.

Kid

To see a child at play in your dreams means that you will be careless in your morals or pleasures, thereby breaking a loved one's heart.

Kidnapper

To dream of a child being kidnapped denotes unexpected loss, especially in new endeavors. If the child is recovered at the end of the dream, disaster can be averted.

Killing

To dream that you see someone trying to kill another, without success, denotes that you will receive money. To dream that you kill another in self-defense, or kill an animal under similar conditions, denotes victory to the dreamer.

King

To dream that you see a king denotes that you are struggling in the wrong direction. For you to dream that you meet a king denotes forgiveness for your faults. To have a long conversation with a king implies a conspiracy undermining your efforts from those you trust.

Kiss

To dream of kissing the hand of anyone speaks of friendship and good fortune. To see children kissing in your dream indicates many happy events. To kiss your sweetheart in the dark relates dangers resulting from improper meetings. For you to dream of kissing a strange woman speaks of loose morals and deceptive honesty. To dream of kissing illicitly relates to pastimes that may end dangerously by giving expression to sexual appetites. To dream that you are being kissed by someone you are trying to avoid means a minor illness to the dreamer.

Kitchen

To see someone cooking in the kitchen suggests you need to

examine your eating habits. If particular kinds of foods such as fish or fowl are sumptuously displayed, your system may benefit from consuming more of these. If, however, what is cooked appears unpalatable, avoid those particular foods, as they may act adversely on your system.

Kite

To dream that you are flying a kite denotes extravagance or poor judgment in the handling of money matters. Should you fail in making your kite fly means sad disappointment. To see children fly kites denotes happiness and success to the dreamer.

Kitten

To see many kittens indicates annoyances and small things that will need your attention. It will take an organized attitude and set of actions to cope with them. To see a single kitten that draws your sympathy indicates someone will need your assistance and you will willingly give help.

Knees

To dream of strong, sturdy knees signifies new duties that you will carry out very well. If the knees are afflicted or crippled in any way, financial worries will befall you. If injured knees are healed in a dream, you will find solutions to financial problems that have been plaguing you.

Knife

To dream of a knife is not good; it refers to quarrels, losses, and separation. To dream that you receive a blow from a knife indicates injuries or violence. To dream that you stab another denotes that you have a poor sense of right and wrong; you should improve this ability.

Knitting

For a woman to dream that she is knitting is good; it implies happiness, peace, and many bright children.

Knots

To see knots and tangled rope, string, or thread suggests many difficulties and problems that will beset your path. To untie a knot successfully indicates the end of a difficult situation or relationship. To tie a knot with happiness denotes a commitment that will be satisfying, whether in romance or in business.

L

"Let not babbling dreams affright our souls."

WILLIAM SHAKESPEARE, English playwright

Laboratory

To dream of being in a laboratory denotes danger of sickness, or energies wasted on useless projects. To dream that you are experimenting with drugs and succeed in discovering a new cure means you will achieve great wealth in your chosen field.

Lace

To dream of lace is good; to see your sweetheart wear it indicates sincerity in love and that everything will end well. To dream that you buy lace means that you will marry a wealthy partner; if married, you will become rich.

Ladder

To dream that you are climbing a ladder denotes good fortune; in fact, great success in business. To dream that you fall from one denotes that your present plans will turn out poorly; many things will arise to discourage you. To climb down a ladder means disappointed efforts and desires that were misdirected from the beginning.

Ladybug

To dream of a ladybug suggests happy pursuits with loved ones.

Lake

To dream that you are alone on a muddy lake denotes many trials and irritations are in store for you in the near future. Should water seep into the boat, but you succeed in scooping it out, you will eventually overcome your difficulties and come out a winner. To dream of sailing on a clear and calm lake with good friends denotes that happiness and success will come to you.

Lamb

To dream of seeing a herd of lambs merrily running about is a happy sign; it denotes an increase in your possessions, and that many good things are awaiting you. To dream of seeing them killed denotes that you must sacrifice pleasures and infatuations if you want to reach your desired goal. To dream of having a pet lamb, or that you are carrying one, denotes great happiness.

Lame

To dream of being lame or seeing someone you know lame denotes scandal and dishonor for the lame person, due to laziness and lack of action.

Lamp

To dream of seeing a lamp burning indicates that your fortune will increase and that you will enjoy domestic happiness. To dream that you drop a lamp means that your plans and hopes are certain to be shattered. To dream of carrying one denotes that you are independent; you prefer to carry out your own ideas, and you seldom take advice graciously.

Land

To dream of owning land or property signifies that you have reached a point of material security in life. If the land is spacious and shows attractive features such as green pastures and streams, you are about to achieve lifelong goals and meet with great success. However, if the land is sparse and poorly kept, it implies that you are making poor use of talents.

Lantern

To dream of seeing a lantern at night in the distance denotes the receipt of unexpected money; if, suddenly, you can no longer see the lantern, then your hopeful plans will take an unfavorable turn.

Lark

To hear this bird singing in a dream signifies easier times to come.

Lasso

To dream of twirling a cowboy's lasso signifies that a sense of adventure and a carefree attitude will be of help to you. To throw a lasso around a steer or a calf indicates effort is required to advance in your life and career. To lasso a horse or pony indicates powerful, but undisciplined, energies and inclinations that can be constructively channeled toward satisfying and successful ends.

Lather

For a man to lather his face denotes a good reputation among associates. For a woman to see a lather of soap denotes that something needs her strong hand to remain on track.

Laughter

To dream that you have been laughing exuberantly means success and many happy associates. To hear children laugh means joy and health to the dreamer; to hear grown people laugh, a speedy break in friendship.

Laurel

To dream of laurel, either as a branch or as a wreath, indicates a victory that will bring honor and success. If this is dreamed prior to the signing of a contract, it suggests an honorable and very favorable deal for you. If the laurel is being held down by some object or is gathering dust, it hints that you are holding on to past successes too long and hindering yourself from new accomplishments.

Law

To dream of being in a courtroom suggests that your work is about to come under scrutiny by others. If the dream shows a judge or jury bringing in a guilty verdict, you will be accused of wrongdoing, whether justly or unjustly. You are advised to conduct all your affairs according to accepted procedures.

Lawn

To see a fine lawn in a dream foretells all things working well in your life. To see a lawn that is dried out, implies an emotional lack in your life. To see weeds on a lawn denotes bad habits and attitudes that mar your character and create many disturbances.

Lawsuits

To dream of being involved in a lawsuit tells of enemies who are trying to influence others against you.

Lawyer

To speak to a lawyer indicates issues that need to be argued and presented to another, lest you suffer ill consequences. To receive praise from a lawyer suggests that a recent thought or argument was well-presented and that you were in the right.

Lazy

To dream of feeling lazy denotes that a business venture will fail through lack of attention to details. To dream of seeing others lazy implies that you will experience difficulty obtaining proper assistance in conducting your business.

Lead (Metal)

To see something made out of lead suggests that a heavy-handed approach will not bring results. If there are lead pipes that carry water in the dream, you are warned at one level to review your spiritual resources, and at another, to question the quality of emotional support others are giving.

Leaf

To dream of a single leaf indicates a small but important success. To see a tree full of healthy leaves indicates a life well spent.

Leaning

To dream of something leaning to one side suggests that forces or people are pressuring you to take a certain direction or action. You are advised to ignore the opinions of others on the issue and make your own decision.

Leapfrog

To dream of playing leapfrog signifies that your career and goals will be marked by friendly competition and rivalry. Or it foretells a joyful relationship.

Leaping

To dream of leaping, demonstrates an active and merry disposition. If you enjoy leaping in the dream, it indicates a period of accelerated activity and success; however, if the leaps are difficult to achieve, it implies that success will be realized, but with strain.

Leather

To dream of seeing piles of leather denotes good fortune and much happiness.

Lecture

To dream of attending a lecture you enjoy means you are about to acquire new knowledge and interests. To dream of attending a lecture you do not enjoy implies harsh words spoken by another. To give a lecture foretells that others will favorably accept your ideas and communications.

Leeches

To dream of leeches implies that enemies will strive to interfere in your affairs. To dream that they are applied to your body denotes an illness, either in yourself or in your family; and also that someone is asking too much of you, and that strong measures are needed to stop it. If your work is all-consuming, it suggests that working too many hours is draining you and needs to be limited. To see leeches on others denotes stress and worry to friends of yours.

Legs

To dream of a woman's legs denotes that you will lose your dignity and act very silly over a dull, uninteresting member of the opposite sex. To dream that you have a wounded leg implies a disappointment, possibly a loss. To dream that you have more than two legs denotes that you are working on more projects simultaneously than you can manage successfully. To dream that you can't use your legs relates to poverty. To see someone who is bowlegged is a signal of financial worries, which can be overcome.

Lemonade

To dream of making lemonade signifies a relaxing time shared with loved ones. To drink lemonade suggests a very healthy emotional and physical life.

Lemons

To dream of seeing lemons on trees denotes that someone you are blaming wrongfully will prove to you that you are mistaken in your accusation. To eat lemons denotes troubles and shattered hopes.

Lending

To dream that you are lending money implies difficulties in meeting your obligations or in paying your bills. To lend articles denotes that you may encounter financial difficulties through overgenerosity. To refuse to lend, means that you will gain wealth and be highly respected by your friends.

Lens

To see the lens of a camera suggests you take a closer look at something, which will bring appreciation.

Leopard

To dream that a leopard attacks you implies that while things look optimistic at present, you will probably experience great difficulties before you reach the end. To dream that you kill one denotes that you will overcome your obstacles. To dream of escaping from one denotes a present difficulty which will turn into joy.

Letters

To write to your friends, or to receive letters from them, means good news, and also that you are interested in literature, especially poetry and drama.

Lettuce
If you eat lettuce only occasionally, to dream of it is a hint that your system requires more of it. Otherwise, if the lettuce is appealing in the dream, it denotes good fortune as well as an invitation that will bring happiness.

Liar
To dream of hearing others call you a liar denotes humiliations through deceitful friends. For you to call another a liar implies that you will regret a former action.

Library
To dream of being in a library suggests success through studiousness and learning, and a professional path in life.

Lice
To dream of lice tells of worry and distress. To dream of seeing them on your body denotes that you will have many irritations and disagreeable obstacles to contend with. To dream of catching them denotes illness.

Licorice
To dream of licorice candy suggests a desire for the playfulness of childhood. A long licorice stick hints at unfulfilled passion.

Lie

To tell a lie and get away with it implies you are succeeding in manipulations, but these will come back to haunt you. If you are lied to in a dream, it is a warning of deception by others, or by a particular person with whom you are engaging in important details.

Lifeboat

To see a lifeboat is a sign that solutions will come, due to the kindness of others. To sit in a lifeboat foretells that a present dire situation will be resolved.

Light

To dream of a light in the distance signifies that the answer to a problem or difficulty is at hand. If a light is dim or small, it suggests that the solution is forthcoming, but that patience is needed till it takes effect. But if the light is bright and strong, it indicates that your life will soon begin anew in a fresh, bright, positive way.

Lighter

To see someone use a lighter to light a cigar or cigarette denotes you will be tempted to take part in detrimental habits.

Lighthouse

To see a lighthouse in a dream suggests that help is at hand for a serious problem. If you are without problems at this time, it implies that you can help others.

Lightning

To dream of seeing lightning foretells of a short period of prosperity. To see lightning strike some object near you means that you will be irritated by jealous people who will gossip about you to your friends.

Lilacs

To dream of lilacs signifies a brief spell of beauty and happiness that is experienced in private.

Lilies

To dream of lilies denotes grandeur, power, and ambition; to smell them out of season, egotistical ambition. To see lilies growing with rich foliage implies an early marriage for the young.

Lime

To dream of the lime fruit denotes the beginning of a new interest or period in your life that will be interesting and pleasurable, but will require some adjustment.

Limp

To see someone walk with a limp predicts financial anxieties or emotional pain to come.

Linen

To see linen or handle it in quantities denotes an abundance of riches. To see others dressed in clothes of this fabric denotes happy news relating to money matters.

Lion

To dream of a lion denotes that you possess strength of character and great determination. To dream that you conquer a lion denotes a victory over temptation. To dream of a cage of lions denotes that your success depends largely on your own personal efforts. To dream of being frightened by a lion is a warning to be very careful in order to avoid potential danger. To dream that you are defending others from a lion and succeed foretells that you will definitely outsmart your enemies.

Lips

To dream of thick lips is a warning to fight against your low moral character. To dream of sweet, natural lips denotes harmony and an abundance of living necessities.

Liquor

To dream that you are drinking hard liquor denotes that you will have many so-called friends hanging on to you for selfish purposes; also, women of a questionable character will try to win your affections.

Lizards

To dream of lizards denotes unpleasant confrontations with enemies. To dream of killing one signifies that you may regain your honor. To dream that one crawls up your clothes means that you will learn of bad reports from friends whom you sincerely trusted.

Loan

To dream of receiving a loan denotes a need to learn to ask for help. To give a loan graciously foretells aiding another in a time of need. It will be repaid. To give a loan with reservation or negative feelings signifies that the help given will be neither appreciated nor repaid.

Lobsters

To dream of lobsters is a happy omen. To see them foretells riches and abundance of wealth. To dream that you eat them means you will be insulted due to your pushy, overfriendly behavior in a public place.

Lock

To dream of a lock is an omen of something that will not work out as you wish it to, no matter what you do. To see something unlocked in a dream signifies the clearing of the way to something that had previously been blocked.

Locket

For an unmarried woman to dream that she receives a locket denotes an early marriage and many happy children. For her to dream that she loses a locket means great sadness is in store for her.

Locksmith

To dream of summoning a locksmith indicates the inability to carry out what you begin, thus losing opportunities for progress.

Locomotive

To dream of a locomotive implies that you are restless and

fond of travels; and if the locomotive is operating, your ambition will be realized. To see one demolished warns of distress and many disappointments.

Logs

To see large, long logs shows that materials needed for success are available. To burn a log in a fireplace denotes a good home life. To dream of a stack of logs suggests that strength is available to help you through a period of trouble. To see a log cabin in a dream implies that you should look toward a simpler lifestyle in order to untangle yourself from difficult conditions.

Looking Glass

To dream of a looking glass is not a good omen. It generally brings about some undesirable news relating to you plans, often disagreements in the family circle.

Loom

To dream that you are weaving on a loom signifies that your life's partner will be a thrifty one, and many happy things are to be expected.

Lord's Prayer

To dream of saying the Lord's Prayer implies that your strongest vocation would be in the mental health field, and you should concentrate your efforts in pursuing this type of career where you can help others.

Loss

To dream of a loss of some valuable item, such as a watch or ring, etc., implies that you will regain as much or more than your loss amounted to. To dream of the loss of money would be similarly significant. To dream that you are losing part of your clothing denotes that you will host a large party, or perhaps deliver a speech in public, or attract attention in a similar way.

Love

To dream that your love is not reciprocated implies that you will probably feel gloomy over some conflicting deal, thus causing you to become very undecided, not knowing which way to go, or what to do. If it relates to business, listen to your first impulse; if it relates to marriage, think carefully, not impulsively. To dream that you love an animal denotes happiness with what you possess and that you are easily satisfied.

Lucky

To dream of being lucky means your wishes will be realized and your ambition achieved.

Luggage

To dream that you have lost your luggage foretells troubles in speculations, and possible family dissension. To the young and unmarried, it means troubles in love.

Lump

To dream of a lump on the body suggests unexpressed creativity that desperately needs expression, lest frustration and an unfulfilled life lead to illness.

M

"Existence would be intolerable if we were never to
dream."

ANATOLE FRANCE, French writer

Macaroni

To dream of seeing macaroni in large quantities denotes that
you are inquisitive and will accumulate some money. To
dream of eating it, as a rule, refers to small losses, usually in
the matter of money.

Machinery

To see large machinery in action amid good feelings denotes
industry that will be rewarded. If you are unhappy at the sight,
it indicates overwhelming forces that rule your life.

Mad Dog

To dream of mad dogs denotes that you will be greatly
annoyed by enemies who will try their utmost to implicate
you in some scandal. If you kill a dog that suffers with rabies,
you may succeed in overcoming their efforts.

Madness

To dream that you suffer from mental illness, and that you are acting irrationally in public, implies that there is sickness ahead of you; you should avoid carelessness relating to catching cold. To see others suffering with mental illness denotes fickle friends.

Maggots

To dream of maggots suggests you need to forgive a situation, even if you were wronged.

Magician

To dream of a conjurer or magician denotes deceit. To dream of seeing a magician performing means you will travel extensively and that you possess keen observational skills. To dream of being a magician denotes that you are extremely fond of the supernatural; something that seemed impossible will come about easily.

Magpie

To dream of this sister bird to the crow indicates quarrels that will cause bitter feelings not easily forgiven. Further, the dreamer is cautioned to be very careful about behavior after such a dream.

Maid

To dream that you are a maid or a servant suggests that an attitude of service toward others would enhance your potential for success. To dream that you are being served by a maid or servant, and enjoying it, is a warning that material things are seducing you from your real goals and potential in life.

Mail

To dream you work at the post office indicates a need to cooperate with others in order to expedite matters. To receive a large quantity of mail denotes advice you are resisting, but would be advised to consider. To receive a single letter that brings happiness indicates a communication that will bring good news.

Man

To dream of a man with a fine physique tells of great satisfaction and joy brought about through rich possessions. To dream of a man with an angry expression implies that you will face many disappointments and problems.

Manager

To dream you manage the affairs of others indicates the ability to take on responsibility and achieve progress in your career.

Manure

To dream of manure hints you are rejecting something in your life that could be of use. If, in the dream, the manure is being applied to some crop or around a plant, it implies that something that appears bad, or not to be working, will in time turn around and become a winning factor.

Manuscript

To dream that you are working on a manuscript and succeed in finishing it denotes that your ambition will be reached; but to dream of an unfinished manuscript denotes disappointments. To dream that you have a manuscript returned foretells of unpleasant criticism of your actions.

Map

To dream of studying a map, or looking up some location, implies that you may soon contemplate a change. To dream that you can't locate the place you are looking for denotes a disappointment.

Marbles

To dream that you are playing marbles denotes that something will occur shortly which will take you back to your childhood's happy days.

Mariner

To dream that you are a career mariner denotes many pleasure trips for the dreamer, and many visits to foreign countries as well.

Marjoram

To see or use the herb marjoram in a dream suggests that you will soon partake of a delightful event or holiday.

Market

To dream of joyfully going to an outdoor farmer's market foretells a coming period of prosperity, rest, and joy.

Marksman

To dream of shooting an arrow or gun and hitting a target denotes you are on track with the development of your career. If a decision is involved for a project, you will successfully conclude it.

Marriage

To dream of planning a marriage denotes that happy times are in the offing. To dream of being married portends unexpected dangers. To see a marriage means sickness and depression. To marry an ugly person predicts death or some serious disaster; a handsome person, joy, happiness, and great advantages. To marry your own wife indicates great profit. To marry a virgin denotes honor without profit. To marry one's sister suggests serious complications. To marry a servant means that others are trying to deceive you.

Marsh

To see a marsh, or attempt to cross it, suggests an unhappy emotional situation for which there is no instant solution. To be lost in a marsh hints that you need the help of another in order to resolve the situation.

Martyr

To dream of suffering martyrdom in a good cause foretells of honors and public testing of character.

Mask

To dream of wearing a mask indicates you are playing a role that is not becoming to you. To see a mask suggests others are hiding their true nature from you.

Mason

To dream of a mason at his duties means a promotion or elevation in your social circumstances and those with whom you associate will now be more agreeable than before. To dream of seeing a body of men belonging to the order of masons, dressed in full uniform, speaks that too many are depending upon you.

Masquerade

To dream of attending a masquerade ball suggests you are in a career or a situation that does not suit you, and you should consider a change.

Massacre

To see a massacre foretells much emotional turmoil, which only professional help can ease.

Mast

To see a ship's mast indicates that career goals need to be more clearly defined. To climb a mast denotes progress in a career.

Mat

To wipe your feet upon a mat foretells a position of servitude. But if you fulfill this gracefully, it will bring advancement.

Matches

To dream of seeing matches denotes that someone will bring you happiness and contentment. To strike a match means that unexpected good news relating to your business affairs will be coming to you in the future.

Mattress

To dream of a mattress denotes that you will be requested to perform new duties shortly. To dream of sleeping on one denotes that your surroundings will cause you to consider many good ideas.

Mayor

To see a mayor or high official who acknowledges you predicts assistance from someone highly respected. To be elected mayor in a dream predicts the attainment of a position of responsibility through which you can help and influence others.

Meadow

To dream that you are in a meadow indicates that you will accumulate valuable property, and that your married life will be one of joy.

Meals

To dream that you see a meal placed on a table denotes that you will let little things in life interfere with the big things, and thereby waste precious time.

Measles

To see others suffering from measles means that you will be requested to assist at a charitable function. To dream of measles or any childhood disease signifies that worries and problems from your early life will come back to plague you. If the afflicted person in the dream is happy despite the illness, you will overcome the troubles.

Meat

To dream of raw meat implies that trouble and discouragement is ahead of you. To dream of cooked meat denotes that you have a rival for the same thing you wish to attain. To see it decayed and rotted is a sign of sickness and death to you or someone you know. If you dream that meat being served to you is cooked rare, to one who likes it that way, it predicts a pleasurable experience. But to one who dislikes rare meat, it is a warning to watch for inadequate preparations of something important. If the meat is well-done, and that is the way you like it, you will soon enjoy the fruits of your labor. If you dislike it well-done, it predicts that something is past due.

Medal

To dream of wearing a medal suggests that acting courageously will bring you honor. To receive a medal foretells of acknowledgment for something that took great effort.

Medicine

To dream that you are taking medicine with difficulty foretells troubles and distress. If it tastes good, it foretells an ailment that you will soon outgrow.

Melon

To dream of melons denotes that you are ridiculing your best friend, making your friend doubt you and your friendship. To dream of eating melon denotes that you judge too quickly; attitude is what will determine your life.

Menagerie

To dream of visiting such a place denotes trouble. If you are single and jealous, it denotes that you will be miserable during your married life.

Mending

To dream of mending an old garment denotes that you will never try to take advantage of any trust again. If you are an honorable person, you will try to correct the mistakes you have made. To dream of fixing clean garments denotes that you will make some gains in the way of a speculative nature.

Mercury

To see silvery streams of liquid mercury denotes changing circumstances that will not benefit you, unless you are in the field of communications. If you have not yet settled on a career, it indicates that more practical thinking toward one direction is required.

Mermaid

To see a mermaid in a dream signifies unusual occurrences soon to take place in your life. It also indicates that you have creative talents.

Merry

For the unmarried dreamer, to dream of feeling merry and lighthearted denotes that a distinguished foreigner wants an introduction with you to propose marriage. For the married dreamer, success and increases of wealth are coming soon.

Message

To receive a message hints at missing information you require in order to do something. To send a message denotes a communication you urgently need to give in order to succeed.

Messenger

To dream of a messenger predicts changes.

Meteor

To see a meteor denotes an unexpected appearance of people and prospects, which can be used to your advantage.

Mice

To dream of being in a room with mice speaks of family troubles and friends who are insincere. It also denotes that business may take a change for the worse. To dream of letting the mice escape implies that you will certainly outsmart your enemies. To dream of feeling a mouse in your clothing denotes that your so-called friends are actually trying to cause trouble for you.

Midwife

To dream of a midwife forebodes that an illness is threatening you, which will bring you almost to death's door. Extreme care should be exercised regarding your physical condition after a dream of this nature.

Milk

To dream that you are drinking milk is a very good dream. It speaks of peace, plenty, and many pleasure trips. To dream of spilling milk relates to slight unhappiness in the home, usually brought about by continually finding fault with one another. To see a quart of milk means either that your body could use more calcium or that the values instilled during childhood should be applied at this time.

Milking

To dream that you are milking, but experiencing difficulty in expressing milk from the cow's udder, denotes that possessions are withheld from you, which you will gain by holding your own and not being persuaded to compromise. If the milk flows without the least amount of effort on your part, good fortune will be forthcoming.

Mine

To dream that you are in a mine, and meet no difficulties in going about it, denotes prosperity. To dream that you are lost in one means danger of failure in business. To dream of owning one denotes trouble instead of anticipated pleasure. To dream that you are working in a mine implies that an enemy is trying to interfere with your plans.

Minister

To dream of a minister foretells that your friends are true and hold you in high esteem. To hear one preach implies that you will assume new duties that will be highly criticized by others.

Mint

To dream of eating a mint candy suggests satisfaction with a completed job or project. To drink mint tea suggests more care be taken with what and how quickly you eat, lest your digestion be affected. To visit a mint where currency is created denotes you have access to ideas and talents that can bring wealth and satisfaction.

Minuet

To dream of dancing the minuet indicates success. To see it danced denotes friends who are congenial and very sincere in their actions toward you.

Mirror

To dream that you are looking into a mirror indicates many discouraging issues. To see others looking into a mirror denotes that they will work their way into your confidence for their own selfish motives. To dream that you break one means bad news bearing the death of a loved one.

Miscarriage

For a childless woman to dream of a miscarriage is an ill omen. It suggests care should be taken with the health and the physical body, especially if a child is desired. If she has just begun a new romance, it predicts she will have cause to end it.

Miser

To dream that you see a miser counting a stack of money usually relates to an increase of your own money. To dream that you are miserly speaks of unhappiness from those who have tremendous egos.

Mist

To dream of mist suggests emotional happiness. But if there is a decision to be made regarding a business dealing, it is a signal to wait before making it so that hidden factors may come to light.

Mistletoe

To dream of mistletoe predicts playful and joyful relationships, but these will be passing friendships only.

Mistreatment

To dream you are treated badly by someone, when you expected good treatment, suggests that you think too highly of someone around you. You are advised not to place anyone you know on a pedestal, at least not at this point in time.

Molasses

To see molasses in your dream relates to pleasant activities and many happy surprises. To dream of eating it denotes unhappiness in your love relationship, brought about by the actions of a rival.

Mole

To see a mole on the arm denotes hard work. On the leg, it signifies journeys. A mole on the back, suggests unfulfilled duties that will bring repercussions. On the stomach, it means poor eating habits. But a mole on a woman's face denotes great inner beauty and strength.

Money

To dream that you receive money denotes good business and prosperity. To dream that someone tells you that you will receive money foretells disappointment in money that you expect. To dream of finding it signifies worries, but ultimately the outcome will be profitable. To pay out money means possible losses. To lose it indicates unhappiness in family affairs. To count it, and find an insufficient amount, means troubles in meeting payments. To steal money warns that you must guard your actions. To save money means comfort and prosperity. To forge money portends shame and blame. To dream of swallowing money denotes that reversals in luck may make you greedy. To dream of finding money suggests an end to difficulties, especially if you have had financial problems.

Monkey

To dream of a monkey implies that deceptive business associates will flatter you to advance their own interests. For a young woman to dream of a monkey denotes that her lover may think she is unfaithful; consequently, it would be advisable for her to insist on an early marriage. To dream of caressing a monkey signifies that your confidence will be betrayed by someone you thought was trustworthy and reliable.

Monster

To dream of a monster or an atrocious-looking creature suggests you are not being honest with yourself and are avoiding the truth. You are advised to come to terms with what is being avoided, lest it overcome you and bring misfortune.

Monument

To dream of a historical monument indicates that aspects of your past can be helpful for your future.

Moon

For a wife to dream of seeing the moon in brilliant clarity tells of love and happiness; for a husband, it means a sudden increase in money matters. To see the new moon indicates an advantageous change in business, or new beginnings. A full moon foretells of love.

Mop

To see an unused mop in a dream is a signal that you have avoided basic tasks that interfere with progress. To see a well used mop indicates sticky emotional situations that you get in the middle of and should try to avoid.

Morgue

To dream that you are going through a morgue looking for someone you know implies bad news, likely the death of a relative. To dream of finding many corpses there is a sign that you will be faced with bitterness.

Mortgage

To dream of paying a mortgage means financial troubles ahead of you, which will cause you many unhappy nights of trying to think your way out. To dream of holding a mortgage against another denotes that you have covered the worst period in life relating to money matters.

Mosquito

To dream of killing mosquitoes denotes that you will frustrate the plans laid by your enemies. To see them, or be annoyed by them, you will suffer a loss at the hands of those who are your enemies.

Moss

To see moss growing suggests a settled, happy home life.

Mother

To hear your mother cry means illness either to you or her. To dream of leaving her relates to difficulties in trying to resolve your problems. To dream of her after a long absence denotes reconciliation between you and relatives. To see her dead denotes troubles to you or to your business. If your mother is dead in reality, and you dream of speaking to her, this denotes happy tidings. To hear her call you implies that you are not following the right business. To see her with a haggard and drawn face foretells of disappointment.

Mountain

To dream that you are going along a high mountain, and are compelled to turn back because you cannot cross a sharp precipice, foretells of troubles and annoyances. To dream that you ascend a mountain successfully implies that you will rise to wealth and prominence. If you fail to reach the top, you may look for reverses. You must be more firm and determined and the future will be brighter.

Mourning

To dream that you are dressed in mourning, or see others so dressed, is a sign of an early wedding in your family, or of a near relative, and you will be asked to help in making the necessary arrangements.

Mousetrap

To dream of a mousetrap indicates coming to terms with something that has been eating away at you. It can also be a signal of slyness around you. Be wary, but not sly yourself.

Mouth

To dream of a beautiful mouth denotes a talent for speaking

and communicating, especially at this period of your life. If the mouth is misshapen or the wrong size, it implies that you are not communicating fully or properly with others, which will bring trouble.

Mud

To dream that you see others covered with mud signifies that you will meet a very boring person. To walk in mud means that you will lose confidence in someone you trusted in the past. To dream of having mud on your clothes means others are gossiping about you.

Muffins

To dream of baking muffins indicates a desire to interact with loved ones and family. To eat a muffin with gusto denotes a loving relationship. To eat a muffin reluctantly, and with little appetite, signals the end of a relationship.

Mug

To dream of drinking from a mug indicates a relaxed life that is working well. To see a shaving mug and shaving materials refers to the need to acquire a new image, both physically and otherwise.

Mule

To dream of a mule denotes that you will be irritated by the mental stupidity of others. To ride one denotes that you will be very worried in your daily activities. To be kicked by a mule speaks of change and disturbance in love and marriage.

Murder

To dream of seeing a murder committed means that you will have to face many immoral acts caused by others; also, that you may learn of the violent death of someone you know. To dream that you are committing murder implies that you are doing something that will ultimately result in losing your reputation. To dream that you are being murdered means that others are secretly trying to steal what rightfully belongs to you.

Museum

To dream of visiting a museum indicates the need to examine past successes and beauties in your life, as a way to mend present disturbances. To work in a museum suggests you need to be more appreciative of the qualities in others.

Mushrooms

To dream of mushrooms predicts that a failure will turn into a success as facts come to light. To eat them denotes special events that will be pleasing.

Music

To dream of soft music means prosperity and great happiness. Loud, unpleasant music denotes friction in your home life; tact is required in order to cope with it.

Mustache

To dream of a large, fine mustache, when in reality you have none, denotes strength and health.

Mystery

To dream that you are involved in some mysterious affair denotes that you will be urged and pestered by strangers to do something that will result in many complications.

Mythology

To dream of an ancient god or goddess is an empowerment and encouragement to follow your own inclinations.

N

"It takes a lot of courage to show your dreams to someone else."

ERMA BOMBECK, American humorist

Nagging

To dream of nagging someone implies you need to get on with something left undone in your life. To dream of being nagged suggests that you are resisting something that will do you good.

Nails (Fingernails)

To dream that you have long nails means great profit. To dream that they are cut very short denotes trouble, dishonor, losses, and family difficulties. To see fingernails torn off means great unhappiness, illness, and losses in the family circle.

Nails (Of Iron)

To dream of rusty nails forebodes illness and decline of business; a lot of nails foretells that you will have many strenuous duties to perform.

Nakedness

To dream that you suddenly discover your nudity, and are desperately trying to cover yourself, denotes humiliations resulting from overindulgence in sexual activities. It is a warning to control those desires. To see yourself nude refers to unwise associates which may prove disastrous. For a man to dream he is running and suddenly loses his clothes denotes trouble from a woman he dislikes who is trying to force her attentions on him or ruin his reputation to her female friends. To dream of seeing others nude denotes that scheming persons are trying their utmost to influence you to join them in their corrupt plans.

Name

To see a written name in a dream is a signal that this person will be of importance to your future path. To hear your name called is a signal from your soul or higher self to pay attention to your inner journey as well as life's material needs.

Napkin

To dream of a clean napkin denotes honorable conduct that will be rewarded. A soiled napkin indicates ailments and sorrow.

Nausea

To dream of someone feeling nauseous or queasy suggests that more anxiety is being created by some situation that you are not acknowledging. If actual upset stomachs are occurring, it is a hint that a medical consultation would be wise.

Navel

To dream of your navel being painful or swollen refers to unpleasant news relating to your father or mother, and the danger of death according to the amount of pain experienced. If the dreamer has neither father nor mother, it relates to suffering and sorrows from the loss of an inheritance.

Navy

To dream of anything relating to the navy usually refers to long trips, victorious undertakings, and joyful recreations. To dream of a dilapidated navy foretells of many struggles and untruthful friends.

Necklace

To dream of losing a necklace means sorrows due to early bereavement. For a woman to dream that she receives a necklace implies many happy gifts from her husband and many joyful hours in the home.

Need

To dream that you are in need indicates that you must be careful or you may make some unwise investment that will have a distressing end. To dream of seeing others in need denotes that you will suffer unexpectedly through showing excessive charity.

Needle

To dream of using a needle is generally an indication of quarrels, which will cause you self-pity because no one will sympathize with you. To find a needle means useless worrying. To dream of threading a needle forebodes that you will be annoyed by the problems and unhappiness of others.

Negligee

To see a beautiful negligee is a signal of delightful love and passion to come. If it is red, embers of love will burn very bright, but may not be long-lasting. If it is a soft hue, love and passion will last. For a woman to dream of wearing a plain nightgown indicates peacefulness. If it is ornate and flamboyant, it indicates a desire to please another, but warns of obstacles in doing so.

Neighbors

To dream of seeing your neighbor shows much time will be wasted in idle gossip. Should the neighbor appear sad and troubled, this denotes dissension that will be lasting and bitter, and neither you nor your neighbors will care to humble yourselves to make up.

Nephew

To dream of seeing your nephew foretells dangerous rivals in both affection and business. To experience difficulties with a nephew implies that you will have great obstacles in adjusting to disagreeable surroundings.

Nervousness

If you are nervous in a dream, it means you are letting anxieties overtake you, and need to find a way to relax in the face of life's pressures. If others are reaching out to you in some way, it indicates that help or advice from others will assist you in lessening stress.

Nest

To dream of finding one, or to see one that is empty, denotes a bankrupt business. To dream of finding a hen's nest relates to domestic affairs such as contentment; also, that you will be blessed with many happy and healthy children. To dream of a nest containing bad eggs means a disappointment is in the offing.

Net

To dream of a net underneath you indicates that in a difficult situation you will receive support from others that will protect you. To be trapped in a net denotes a powerful adversary who may succeed in outsmarting you, unless you avoid confrontations with this person.

Nettles

To dream of treading on nettles or being stung by them denotes that you are restless and never satisfied with your position, always complaining of your luck. You must be more firm and determined and things will look brighter.

Newspaper

To dream that you are reading a newspaper indicates deceit, lies, and that you will be accused of cheating in your activities, which will endanger your good reputation to a certain extent.

New Year

To dream of a New Year celebration signifies new beginnings. If there is a happy atmosphere, the beginning will in time bring good fortune.

Night

To dream that you are walking at night denotes that unexpected hardships may be in store for you in your immediate plans; but should you see the night vanish before you, your troubles will disappear and be resolved.

Nightingale

To dream of a nightingale singing sweetly portends of happiness in a relationship. If a nightingale appears in the dream of a newlywed, it signals that the birth of child is forthcoming.

Nightmare

To have a nightmare while sleeping means that disagreements and worries will confront you. For the unmarried, it means disappointments are in store.

Noise

To hear a peculiar noise in your dream foretells unpleasant news. Should the noise succeed in awakening you, a change for the better can be expected.

Noodles

To dream of a large, inviting dish of noodles suggests you can nurture and heal others. To see a dish of noodles that is revolting hints that you are eating too many starchy foods.

Noose

To see a noose hanging empty from a high place denotes an escape or reprieve from consequences that would have been very unpleasant. To see a noose placed around your neck indicates an overwhelming fear of consequences. To end these fears, you may need to leave a situation behind.

Nose

To dream of seeing your own nose signifies that you have more friends than you think; you are admired for your character and sympathetic nature. Your love of nature is exceedingly strong.

Nosebleed

To see a nose bleeding indicates an unexpected affront that will be painful and distressing. It also indicates a period of great pressure that will require calmness.

Numbers

To dream of numbers and to be unable to remember them denotes that business will cause you uneasiness due to its unsettled condition. To remember numbers implies good fortune is in store for you in the future.

Nun

If a woman dreams of a nun, it means widowhood, or perhaps

a separation from her lover. For a man to dream of a nun denotes that he is more concerned about material wealth than about his spiritual self.

Nurse
To dream of nursing a child denotes an illness to some member of the family. To dream that you are a nurse implies that you will occupy a position of responsibility and trust.

Nursery
If a childless young couple dreams of a nursery, it foretells the beginnings of a family soon to come. Otherwise, a nursery is a signal of new projects and interests you will be involved with for many years.

Nutmeg
To dream of adding the spice nutmeg to a recipe foretells an ending to a difficult situation, brought about by tact and good will.

Nuts
To see nuts in their shells denotes a puzzle that needs to be solved. If successful in cracking them, the answers will be forthcoming. To see a full bowl of shelled nuts indicates abundance will be yours. However, to eat nuts signifies you are accepting that which is untrue.

Nut Tree
To dream of a nut tree laden with nuts foretells great success,

but it will be achieved only through labor and persistence. To dream of gathering nuts and storing them is an indication to use your income wisely.

Nymphs

To dream of nymphs bathing in clear water denotes festive parties with good friends enjoying many delicacies, and dishes of specialty foods being served. To see them out of water would denote a disappointment.

"To me dreams are part of nature, which harbors no intention to deceive but expresses something as best it can."

CARL JUNG, Swiss psychologist

Oak

To dream of seeing a tall oak with many leaves means riches and happiness and that you will live to a ripe old age. To see an oak tree full of acorns speaks of an elevation in your status. For the lover to dream of oaks refers to an early marriage to his betrothed.

Oars

To pull the oars of a rowboat means you will have to exert yourself greatly to reach your ambitions. To find only one oar in a boat suggests you have need of a partner before your life can proceed smoothly.

Oasis

To see an oasis signals a restful interlude in an otherwise

demanding or difficult period. Seeing an oasis also can refer to inner resources that get you through difficulties.

Oath

To dream of taking an oath is an invariable sign of complications and irritations in your immediate future.

Oatmeal

For you to dream of oatmeal heralds many happy conditions; to eat it, good health to enjoy your good fortune.

Obedience

To see someone obey an order or directive in a dream shows a need to cooperate with those in authority.

Obesity

To dream of a very obese person warns of barriers to manifesting your best creative energies. It warns you to be very honest in assessing the use of your talents.

Obituary

To dream of reading a friend's obituary implies that unpleasant news will soon reach you. To dream of writing one means many boring duties will be delegated to you.

Obsession

To obsess over something in a dream signifies that something has become too important to you, and that it will end in disappointment.

Occultist

To dream of an occultist denotes that you will be forced to acknowledge an error you've made and to apologize for it. To dream that you are studying or going to become an occultist means that you will be rewarded in some way for the kindness you have shown to others.

Ocean

To see the ocean calm in your dream is good. For the businessman, it denotes splendid remuneration. For the young, it means they will fall in love. To dream of being on a stormy sea refers to troubles in business and disagreements in the household. To watch a rough sea from the shore implies that enemies are talking disrespectfully about you. To dream you are in the middle of an ocean signifies emotional turmoil. However, if at the end of the dream you find yourself at the shore, the turmoil will resolve. To swim in the ocean denotes making your way successfully through difficult emotional situations.

Octopus

To see this sea creature with eight long arms is a signal you are reaching for too much in life at once, and need to scale down your expectations and pace your goals.

Oculist

To dream of consulting an eye doctor foretells that you dislike your occupation; a change would be advisable.

Odor

To be exposed to an unpleasant odor is a warning of trouble arising from things in your past. To dream of smelling a pleasant smell in a dream denotes help from spiritual sources.

Offense

To dream that your actions have offended the sensitive feelings of others predicts many obstacles in your way before your ambition is achieved. To dream that others offend you signifies that others are criticizing your actions unjustly, which will cause you to lose your temper.

Offering

To dream of making a generous donation for the benefit of the church signifies a desire to return to religion. To make a small contribution denotes that after you have tried to lead an honest life, you will return to your former corrupt way of living.

Office

To dream of an office or work environment suggests that responsibilities need attention.

Officer

To dream that an officer enters your home or place of business to serve legal papers denotes unpleasant and discouraging news from those whom you expected to bring good news.

Offspring

To dream of your own offspring signifies happiness and

strong parental love. To dream of seeing the offspring of animals predicts energies that will bring about prosperity.

Oil

To dream of spilled oil denotes irreparable losses. To see it on yourself denotes profit and gain. In large quantities, your excess in pleasure may cause you suffering.

Ointment

To dream of using an ointment signifies the healing that you give to another.

Old Age

To see yourself as an aged person signifies longevity. It hints that you can afford to be patient in life, because much still awaits you.

Old Man

To see an old man who gives good advice or support signifies much help is yours when you need it.

Old Woman

If a woman dreams of an old woman, it signifies that an alliance with a female will further her affairs. If a man dreams of an old woman, it indicates that he needs to cultivate artistic pursuits. To see an old woman who knows the answers shows that experience will be your teacher.

Olives

To dream of olives is a good omen. To eat them means many true friends; to gather them means many favorable results in business. To dream of olives on a tree denotes peace, liberty, dignity, and the attainment of desires. To dream of olives in a cocktail indicates a need to distinguish what is wholesome and helpful from that which is not.

Olympic Games

To see the Olympics or any part thereof in a dream denotes the need to be disciplined and to work hard; these traits will pay great dividends within four years.

Omelet

To dream of preparing an omelet indicates a talent for turning plain materials into special objects and outcomes. To eat an omelet signals an increase in strength that will empower you.

Omen

To see a lucky charm such as a rabbit's foot in a dream signals good fortune and a good outcome. To see a more sinister omen such as a shrunken head or a voodoo doll denotes fears and anxieties caused by others that will impede progress. If you overcome these fears, you will meet success.

Omnibus

To dream of riding through the streets in an omnibus or bus implies that your friends are doing things that you do not approve of, which ultimately may cause the loss of your friends.

Onions

To dream of seeing many onions relates that your success in life will bring about much envy and jealousy. To eat them is good; it means overcoming obstacles.

Opal

To see this lovely gem in a dream denotes special charm you can draw on to achieve your aims.

Opera

To dream of seeing an opera predicts many good friends; through their influence, you will attain much that is good in life. To appear in an opera predicts hatred and jealousy, due to your dignified and independent ways.

Opium

To dream of this drug predicts that others are trying to injure you in your prospective plans through devious methods of which you are unaware.

Opulence

To dream of imagined opulence signifies lack of strength of character and no determination. The dreamer should cultivate the application of the ideas of effort and continuity, and the power of decision-making.

Oranges

To dream of seeing oranges on trees is an excellent omen. It means happiness and prosperity. To eat them generally refers to illness, or news of a convalescent. To dream of buying them implies that complications will grow into profit.

Orator

To dream of becoming enthused by an orator's eloquence denotes that an appeal will be made to you for a contribution, which you will thoroughly believe due to the sincerity in the tone of voice. For a woman to dream of being in love with an orator denotes that she is lazy, impressionable, sentimental, and spoiled.

Orbit

To see a spaceship lifting into orbit relates to a new idea that will be well received and lead to success.

Orchard

To dream of passing through a fruit-bearing orchard predicts happiness and prosperity. To pass through a barren orchard indicates trouble gaining a coveted object in life. To dream of gathering fruit means that success will be achieved in your business and personal endeavors.

Orchestra

To dream of hearing an orchestra play means that things will greatly pick up in the near future and remain very encouraging thereafter. To dream of playing in an orchestra means your sweetheart or wife will bring happiness into your life.

Orchid

To see this delicate flower in a dream is a very fortunate sign; it shows unique qualities will bring success and acclaim.

Organ

To dream of playing an organ predicts much happiness and a comfortable life; also, that your position in life is predestined. To hear an organ played with selections that appeal to the heart means lasting and devoted friendship. To hear doleful music, you will soon learn of events that will sadden you.

Organizing

To see someone organizing many details in a dream is a hint to carefully attend to details, or else risk problems.

Orgasm

To experience orgasms in a dream denotes unfulfilled passion. Or, it may refer to some nonsexual experience that will turn out to be extremely satisfying. To crave orgasm but not achieve it in a dream is a sign of unrequited love.

Ornaments

To dream of receiving an ornament denotes a contemplated change that should be carried out. To give an ornament warns you to guard your extravagance. To lose an ornament denotes the loss of a friend or something material.

Orphan

To see an orphan in a dream means you feel unloved and unsupported. To adopt an orphan foretells that a kindness you do for someone will benefit them greatly.

Oscar

To dream of watching the Academy Awards, or any awards ceremony, implies that your creative efforts, if pursued, could bring much success.

Ostrich

To dream of this bird denotes that you will gain possessions through your unrestrained kindliness and diplomacy, mingled with deceptiveness that you will ultimately have to deal with. To catch an ostrich foretells of travels and interviews with famous people.

Otter

To see this water mammal swim predicts you will successfully navigate an emotional situation.

Outburst

To dream of showing an outburst of a positive emotion is an encouragement to display your feelings more spontaneously. To show negative outbursts suggests you should be more guarded in displaying feelings.

Outcast

To dream of seeing an outcast foretells the ending of a

friendship. To be the outcast indicates you will be rejected by peers or acquaintances, whether fair or not.

Outlaw

To dream of meeting an outlaw represents an inclination to set your own standards and rules in your life. If the outlaw is clean-cut and pleasant, it is an encouragement to do so. If he is unshaven and coarse, it is a signal to conform at this time, rather than to rebel against existing standards.

Oven

For a woman to see an oven overheat denotes many distant friends, which ultimately may cause her to relocate. If a woman dreams that she is baking, it means slight disappointments in her life will lead to unhappiness and restlessness.

Owl

To dream of hearing the sounds of an owl in the distance is a sign that grief will soon shatter the nerves of the dreamer. To see an owl implies that enemies are watching for advantageous opportunities. Take careful stock of something, because hidden factors need to come to light. If the owl hoots, it suggests that communications with others will help you to uncover what is undermining the project.

Ox

To dream of seeing a fat ox predicts that good times and happiness are near at hand, while dreaming of a lean ox means poor times and little reward for your efforts. To see them fight is an indication of an early quarrel.

Oxygen Mask

To dream of an oxygen mask implies a need to take in more that is fresh and pure, especially of an intellectual nature. To see someone use an oxygen mask in a dream indicates you have feelings of emotional suffocation and restraint that need to be released.

Oysters

To dream of seeing oysters served on the table denotes friendship. To eat them raw is a splendid sign of excellent health and fine success.

P

"We sometimes from dreams pick up some hint worth improving by reflection."

THOMAS JEFFERSON, 3rd U.S. President

Package

To dream of receiving a package unexpectedly is a good omen and indicates help from strangers. To send a package overseas or a long distance suggests a renewed contact with an old friend or distant relative. If your spouse is in the armed forces, it denotes a distant assignment.

Packing

To dream of packing hints at an unexpected trip. Or, it can signify the end of something long-standing, either in career or home life.

Page

To see a page in your dreams denotes that your marriage will turn out to be socially unacceptable. You should make sure the prospective partner is worthy of you before taking the step. To dream that you are a page implies that you will commit some petty theft, which will cause you regret.

Pagoda

To see an Oriental temple signifies you can get in touch with your intuition, whereby quiet moments will bring the answers you need.

Pail

To see a lot of empty pails in your dream predicts an unprosperous condition. To dream that you see a filled pail, or carry a filled pail, denotes that success will be achieved, with all the accompanying pleasures. To dream of a pail full of clean water signifies that you will soon find the answer to a question. If the pail is empty, you will have to continue to wait to resolve the question. If the pail is filled with murky or dirty water or liquid, you are warned that a decision that you are in the process of making will bring an unfortunate result.

Pain

To dream that you suffer pain forebodes unhappiness, and that you will regret some trivial affair not worth bothering about. To see others suffering pain denotes that you are holding onto a mistaken ambition.

Paint

To dream that you are covered with paint denotes that your pride will be hurt through unfair criticism of others. To dream of admiring beautiful paintings means that friends whom you thought sincere don't think too much of you. To dream that you are painting yourself implies energy and vitality wasted on an object that will bring you little or no reward. For a woman to paint a picture predicts that the person she admires adores someone else, and that she will suffer from an unrequited love.

Painter

To dream that you are a painter, or see a painter at work, foretells success in an enterprise that requires creativity, whether in ideas or in art.

Pair

To see a row of identical items, from which you are attempting to pick one item, refers to a serious decision you are in the process of trying to make. If, in the dream, you pick an item, you are on the verge of making a choice. If you do not, the dream is suggesting you need more information before you can decide.

Pajamas

To dream of a pair of pajamas with a blouse top and a pair of pants suggests you should take an easy-going approach with others, and at the same time, assert a strong position.

Palace

To dream that you are in a palace and are delighted with its grandeur denotes that you will attain public recognition during your lifetime. To see one only from the outside foretells of stress, irritations, and jealous rivals that will cause you much suffering.

Pallbearer

To dream that you act as a pallbearer foretells humiliation by the constant accusations of enemies. To see a pallbearer denotes you will make yourself disliked by expressing your opinions. To see several pallbearers in a dream foretells major changes in your life. If the funeral procession is peaceful and orderly, these will be positive changes. If the procession is heavy and filled with gloom, the changes will not be as welcome.

Pallor

To see people especially pale of face in a dream hints at ill health. Or, it suggests little enthusiasm for life.

Palmistry

For a young woman to dream of palmistry denotes that she has strong psychic force and the power to predict good things for others. For a man to dream of palmistry foretells that he has the power to encourage the disheartened to succeed. To dream of having your palms read predicts that, in reality, you have many friends; but openly they may condemn you. Should you dream of reading palms, or that you have read the palm of another, means riches and fame for you. To dream of reading a clergyman's hand denotes that your strong point is in the mental realm, and that you can persuade a crowd better than an individual.

Palm Reader

To dream of a palm reader is an indication that the advice of another will be of help to you, and may come from an unusual person.

Palm Tree

To dream of a palm tree indicates a visit to a warm, exotic climate. Or, it can refer to unusual and exotic ideas that will work for you.

Pampering

To see someone pampered implies a need for self-nurturing, if you are a person who gives little attention to yourself, or that there is too much thought to your own needs.

Pancakes

To dream of making pancakes foretells that your common-sense and thrifty qualities will lead you to good fortune. To eat them implies that a new plan will end profitably.

Panda Bear

To dream of a panda tells you that someone of whom you are uncertain may appear fierce, but is in fact approachable and gentle in nature.

Panic

To see someone panic-stricken denotes your feelings of panic over something. If the dream ends happily, all will end well.

If the ending is uncertain, it is a hint to calm your feelings to avoid an unfavorable outcome.

Panther
To dream of a graceful black panther implies great strength of character that will bring you forward in life.

Pantomime
To dream that you are performing denotes slight unpleasantries that will be a stumbling block for a short period. To see others perform means that some indiscrete friend will reveal your secret.

Pantry
To see a full pantry denotes a life that is full and well-lived. To see an empty pantry suggests you need to create more of a home life and social life.

Pants
For a woman to see a pair of men's pants in a dream indicates that she needs to assert herself more. For a man to dream of a woman's pants suggests that he become less aggressive in demeanor.

Paper
To dream of a piece of paper suggests that something in your life needs to be looked into. If you are writing in the dream, it is an indication that increased communications will advance you in life at this time. If the paper contains figures, you should

examine your financial affairs for hidden factors, which are either liabilities or opportunities.

Paradise

To dream of paradise implies you are in very unpleasant circumstances that you would like to see changed. However, change will come about when you assume more practical and realistic attitudes.

Parallel Lines

To see lines or items aligned in a dream, where their parallel feature is prominent, suggests that two or more issues are closely related and thereby work together.

Paralysis

This is a bad dream in whatever form it may be brought about. It denotes money troubles, suffering, long illnesses, and bitter disappointments to the dreamer. To lovers it predicts affection that turns cold and dies away.

Parasite

To dream of a parasite implies either that others are demanding and receiving too much from you, or that you are doing the same to another.

Parasol

For a married person to dream of a parasol predicts unhappiness that will ultimately bring about disaster. For the unmarried it denotes a desire to flirt and a fondness for admiration.

Parcel

To dream of receiving a parcel implies a surprise from one whom you least expect. To lose one means that an offer will fail to materialize.

Pardon

To dream that you are innocently jailed and seek pardon foretells present troubles that will ultimately prove to your advantage. To dream that your punishment is just means obstacles will lie ahead for you to overcome.

Parents

Should your parents be dead in reality, and appear to you in a dream, this foretells troubles. You must exercise care in the planning of affairs. To dream of living parents and see that they are happy and well denotes fortunate changes. If you are on good terms with your parents, to dream of them is a good sign and denotes health and happiness. Otherwise, it signifies standards that are too high, and which need to be relaxed.

Park

To dream of going through a beautiful park predicts pleasant happenings to the dreamer. To a lover, the park means you will glide smoothly on the matrimonial sea. To stroll through a park usually hints that you need to take time for rest and leisure.

Parka

To see a parka in a dream is a signal that you need to shield yourself from the lack of acceptance from others, which may occur to some extent at this time. Use confidence and draw on inner reserves to do so.

Parking

To see someone park a car or a vehicle signifies that a less hectic schedule will soon be made manifest.

Parking Meter

To see a parking meter suggests that paying your dues for small niceties and requirements is imperative, lest not doing so bring on large, disproportionate consequences of resentment and loss of opportunity.

Parrot

To dream of a parrot means discovering a secret. For the unmarried to dream of owning a parrot, lovers' quarrels may be on the way.

Parsley

To dream of putting parsley in a dish being cooked signifies that something new you are now adding to your life is good for you.

Parting

To dream of an emotional parting from friends implies that little things will annoy you greatly.

Partridge

To dream of this bird foretells intimacy with ungrateful partners.

To kill one means that you possess the power of acquiring, but not accumulating, wealth. To eat one, if you enjoy the taste, foretells enjoyment and success.

Party

To someone in a period of high work demands, a party setting reflects a need for some relaxation and distraction. Otherwise, it foretells an upcoming, pleasurable event.

Passenger

To be a passenger in a car, airplane, or other vehicle suggests you should gracefully go along with changes that will soon enter your life. All things will fall easily into place.

Passion

To dream of a scene of passion foretells of love. If you are not in a relationship, it indicates a need for love that will shortly be fulfilled.

Passivity

To see passivity in a dream indicates you may be depressed or in a situation that you feel is beyond your control. The purpose of the dream is to put you in touch with these feelings so that you may exert yourself and do something to change the situation.

Passport

To dream of being issued a passport signifies new and very different doors will open for you in the near future. To apply for a passport and be granted one is a signal that the changes you see will come to pass. If an official refuses to grant you a passport, either it is not the right time for change, or more learning or experience must first be acquired.

Password

To require a password in order to proceed in a dream suggests that certain knowledge or experience is needed for that to which you aspire. If you have the password, you will achieve your aim.

Paste

To dream of paste on your clothes denotes that those with whom you are dealing are hiding their bad habits in order to win your confidence and gain their selfish purpose through your influence. To dream that you are pasting predicts the matters you thought were settled must be reviewed.

Pastel Colors

To dream of pastel colors suggests a light, gentle approach or touch is appropriate for whatever is at hand.

Pastry

To dream of making a pastry denotes pleasures and profit. To see a pastry denotes that some sly person is seeking to deceive you. To eat it foretells many happy times among friends.

Pasture

To dream of a fine, green pasture signals a peaceful, happy old age. If barren, it warns you to begin to provide for older years.

Patent

To dream that you have conceived a patent denotes that the dreamer seeks, reasons, calculates, and wants positive proof before going ahead. To dream that you tried to receive a patent, but failed, predicts that you reason things to death; you should trust your first impressions more.

Paths

To dream of walking down a wide, well lit, attractive road or path predicts that you are entering a period of life when all will come easily and harmoniously to you. If the path is narrow, crooked, dark, and unattractive, the next period of your life will be fraught with challenge and difficulty.

Patience

To dream of someone acting in a patient manner is a warning to be patient in a situation. But if the scene depicts someone as overly patient, it suggests that you need to take aggressive action to remedy something.

Pattern

To see a pattern showing how to sew a piece of clothing is a signal that you have the creative resources to come up with an original item, which others will want.

Pauper

To dream that you are a pauper refers to sudden and unexpected wealth. To dream of seeing other paupers denotes that you will be requested to offer assistance.

Pavement

To dream that you are walking on pavement that caves in, but are unhurt, denotes that a new business prospect that is an excellent opportunity will soon come your way.

Pawn Shop

To dream that you pawned articles denotes that family problems, which are your fault, are staring you in the face. To redeem a pawned article indicates that many of your efforts were misdirected, but are now on the right track.

Paycheck

To dream of searching for a paycheck indicates either delays in getting a job, or a loss of position. To receive a paycheck indicates a stable income and acquisition of work.

Pea

To dream of a pea denotes small items that add up to important assets. To pick peas suggests patience will be needed. To dream of eating peas, and if they are luscious to the taste, denotes an increase in business with quick profits. To dream of eating them raw would imply problems and disappointments that the dreamer will have to overcome.

Peaches

To dream of eating peaches in season indicates much satisfaction and enjoyment. To dream of them out of season means struggles and disappointment.

Peacock

To dream of seeing one spreading his tail means wealth and indicates a very handsome partner. For a woman to dream that she owns a peacock denotes that she is placing too much confidence in a certain person. Be careful of how much of your past you reveal. To dream of pulling the bird's beautiful feathers denotes that you will fail to obtain a certain object because of your proud spirit.

Peanuts

To dream of unshelled peanuts signifies preparations required before something can be useful. If they are shelled, it means you interact with humble items and activities, and these bring you satisfaction. A large basket of peanuts suggests earnings will accrue slowly.

Pearls

To dream of pearls is a favorable omen. It means excellent business and not much to annoy you. For a girl to dream of receiving a string of pearls from her lover means many good things for her. For her to dream of breaking or losing her pearls would imply deep sadness through misunderstanding.

Pears

To dream of eating pears in season foretells of happiness, particularly if they are sweet. To dream of green or decayed pears means that sickness and disappointment lie ahead.

Pebble

To dream of throwing a pebble into the water indicates a wish or desire that had been unconscious but is now becoming clear, so you can begin to determine how to make it a reality. To have a pebble thrown at you or another is a signal that someone you are ignoring wants to get your attention. Pebbles thrown against a window at night denote a secret love interest.

Peel

To dream of peeling an orange or some other fruit foretells a wonderful surprise—but one that will unfold in stages.

Pelican

To see a pelican in your dream relates to success slowly reached. To dream of catching one means you will divert an enemy before he does much damage to you.

Pen

To see a beautiful pen signifies that what you write can bring good fortune. If the pen is damaged, you are advised not to sign anything of importance at this time.

Penalty

To dream that you are compelled to pay a penalty refers to loss and sickness. To dream that you get off free means honors and distinction. To dream that a penalty will be imposed on you denotes that you will be mixed up in a misunderstanding due to some argument.

Pencil

To sharpen a pencil implies that you are preparing for something you have wanted for a long time. To write with one means temporary conditions now in your life will soon change.

Penitentiary

To dream of being a confined convict denotes that you will have many petty things to annoy you. To escape from one means you will conquer those who are against you. To dream of a penitentiary foretells that you will have disagreeable duties to perform.

Penknife

To dream of opening up a penknife means you need to keep sharp wits about you at this time, as you will need them to meet upcoming situations. To use one to open something refers to using well honed skills to achieve your goals.

Penny

To dream of pennies implies little return on present efforts.

Pension

To dream you receive a pension means the ending of present projects. To seek a pension suggests a desire for less work, and hints that more relaxation would be beneficial.

People

To dream of a crowd of people at a fashionable affair denotes many pleasant things to the dreamer. To dream of a boisterous crowd of people predicts discouraging conditions, perhaps brought about by family problems. To dream of seeing many well-behaved people is always good; to see them otherwise means trouble of some kind.

Pepper

To dream of pepper is not good. It relates to worry, concern, irritation, and a meeting with someone who is difficult to get along with.

Perfume

To dream of perfuming yourself denotes that you will hear many complimentary things said about you. To dream of receiving perfume as a gift predicts many advantages, and that you will associate with people of intelligence. To smell it is always good.

Perjury

To see someone commit perjury in a dream is a warning that you are not being truthful with yourself. If you have not been truthful or are considering fudging the truth in a situation, it is a warning that you may be caught in a lie.

Persian Rug

To dream of walking on a beautiful oriental rug foretells that you will do some of your best work in the coming years, and this will bring you much satisfaction and renown.

Perspiration

To dream that you are perspiring freely denotes that problems troubling you will soon disappear; you will prove to those who have been gossiping about you that you are not as bad as they thought.

Peter Pan

To see this fabled youth from Never-Never Land, who never grows up, suggests that retaining a youthful attitude and state of mind would be beneficial. However, if a single woman dreams of Peter Pan just as she meets a new suitor, it is a warning that the man is immature.

Petticoat

For a young woman to dream that she is losing her petticoat in some public place denotes that her lover is losing interest in her. The woman should be more reserved, and not too obvious about how she feels, in order to keep the man guessing, because he loves to chase something that is difficult to attain. To dream of a petticoat with many contrasting colors means many petty annoyances are going to be faced. To dream of a very rich and expensive petticoat denotes pride and dignity.

Phantom

To dream that a phantom is chasing you, but that you succeed in getting away, denotes joy and freedom from your present worries. If a phantom touches you, this foretells of unpleasant experiences. To see one in black predicts troubles from a woman. To see one running away from you means troubles are at an end.

Pheasant

To dream of this bird denotes great happiness. To kill one denotes that you must fight against a certain temptation. To eat one denotes that your high living and overeating will produce a weak digestive system.

Photocopying

To see something photocopied suggests that continuing the course you are on is beneficial, and that tried-and-true actions and habits will continue to help you.

Photograph

To dream that you are having your picture taken denotes that you will be mistaken for someone else and be very embarrassed. To see pictures denotes happiness. To see yourself in an amusing pose implies that gossips are talking about you. To dream that you are taking photographs predicts that your love for the aesthetic is interfering with daily business concerns.

Physician

For a girl to dream of a doctor implies that she is foolishly thinking of things which may cause trouble for her. To dream that she is sick, and has the doctor, denotes that sorrow is in store for her. For a married woman to dream of a physician denotes that she lacks self-control and imagines illness which does not exist.

Piano

To dream of hearing pleasing piano music denotes joy and

contentment; loud, harsh music, possible family disagreements. For an unmarried woman to dream of playing a difficult piece of music predicts success in love with a disinterested lover.

Pickles

To dream of pickles means misdirected efforts and energy wasted, not liking your present job, but performing your duties just to remain employed or only for a paycheck. To dream of pickles also tells of troubles in love, but not necessarily separation. For a girl to dream of eating pickles denotes many rivals for the person she loves.

Pickpocket

To see a pickpocket in your dream foretells that an enemy will annoy you very much and cause others to misjudge you. To dream of having your own pockets picked denotes that a friend will become an enemy through the spiteful actions of others.

Picnic

To dream that you help to make a picnic a huge success implies an advancement and ultimate fun and success. To dream that your planned activities at a picnic are interrupted for some reason means that your plans will not be completed quite as you would have liked.

Pictures

To dream that you are drawing pictures denotes a lot of hard work with very little profit. To see them means that surprises from unexpected friends are in store for you in the future.

Pies

For an unmarried woman to dream of baking a pie signifies that her love of admiration and her desire to flirt may lead to trouble. To dream of eating pies means that enemies are talking disrespectfully about you.

Pigeons

To dream of pigeons indicates a need to join a group or to fraternize more within groups. If you are about to embark on a journey, it signifies a pleasant trip, with leisurely jaunts through new areas.

Pigs

To see a large pig in a dream implies that you feel guilt or remorse about eating habits, and need to come to terms with consuming either too little or too much. To dream of a sow with a litter of piglets, on the other hand, suggests that you can nurture many around you, and have talents that will benefit society and loved ones. To dream of fat, healthy pigs denotes that your energies will be rewarded. To dream of lean, sickly-looking pigs means a great deal of hard work and efforts that will ultimately prove to be useless.

Pillow

For a woman to dream that she is making a pillow denotes a comfortable, peaceful life, and that she will be surrounded by luxuries. To dream of many beautiful pillows predicts a love for romance and sentiment.

Pills

To dream of taking pills signifies that you accept labels others give you without question. To dream of seeing someone take a pill suggests that help and a solution are at hand, for either an illness or an unhappy situation. To see pills lying about or in a bottle hints you will need to do something you would rather not do.

Pilot

To dream of being a pilot suggests teaching skills and the ability to understand complex situations and ideas. To see a pilot in the cockpit of an airplane implies the ability to rise above unpleasant situations.

Pimples

To dream of having pimples on your body means great wealth, both in real estate and personal property. To see them on others is an indication of disgust, due to the gossip that is being repeated by others.

Pineapple

To dream of a pineapple predicts an experience that will have a duality about it: it will be pleasant and yet difficult.

Pine Tree

To dream of a pine tree or pine needles denotes you are in need of rest, both physical and mental. You are advised to take a period of relaxation in an outdoor setting where there are trees.

Pins

To dream that you will not allow someone to prick you with a pin denotes a surprise. For example, you will receive a great deal more than what you originally asked for, or expected. To dream of swallowing a pin denotes that unforeseen circumstances will result in an unpleasant situation. To see pins used in sewing is an indication of patience required for a situation. To see someone brandishing a pin as if it were a threatening weapon foretells that unkind words, likely undeserved, will be directed toward you.

Pipe

To dream that you follow a loved one by crawling through a long, dark, rusty sewer pipe, and experience a smothered feeling, denotes a bitter disappointment. To dream of smoking a pipe means that you will meet an old acquaintance whom you thought was angry with you. To see a lot of old broken iron pipes means poor business.

Pirates

To dream of pirates in a happy setting implies a need for new horizons and adventure. However, to see pirates creating havoc signifies that you are stepping out of bounds in life, and will rebound badly.

Pistol

To dream of shooting a pistol denotes that you will apologize to someone for a false accusation you made based solely on something you heard. To dream of pistols in general foretells difficulties.

Pit

To dream of someone falling into a pit foretells an unexpected turn of events that will throw your life into chaos, either mentally or materially. You are cautioned to accept what transpires with tranquility, for it will pass.

Pitcher

To dream of a pitcher denotes a loss, generally due to your own carelessness, sometimes due to others. To dream of a broken pitcher refers to the loss of friends.

Pity

To see something in a dream that evokes your pity hints at a need to be more responsive and sensitive to the trials and tribulations of others.

Plague

To dream of a place where a plague is rampant implies poor business terminating in thorough discouragement. Even the home may be shattered due to poor business. To dream that you are afflicted with the plague denotes that you will become confused mentally over conditions. This is a warning that you must not lose self-control.

Plane

To dream you are on a plane denotes that your efforts will be rewarded and your ambition achieved. To see others working on a plane foretells good business conditions.

Planet

To dream of a heavenly body denotes joyful tidings.

Plank

To dream of walking across a plank safely foretells that a project will be successful. To dream of crossing a rotten plank and having it break means unhappiness lies ahead.

Plants

To dream of healthy, potted houseplants indicates that your life is harmonious and peaceful. If the plants show deformity or illness, examine close associations for unspoken problems which, if not mended, could ruin the relationship. If the dream is of large, healthy, tree-size plants, either indoor or outdoor, you will prosper in the months to come.

Plaster

To see plastered walls suggests support from others is not as solid as it could be. To see a plaster cast on a body part warns of shortcomings and unexpected tribulations that can cause delays in your career or a project.

Plate

To see an empty plate suggests a lack of meaningful activity in your life, but this can changed. To break a plate warns of antagonism or sharp words that can ruin an opportunity or an employment situation. To see a plate filled with luscious fruit or foods points to successful outcomes of present activities.

Play

To dream of attending a play is a sign of short-lived pleasures. For the unmarried to dream of a play denotes that their sweethearts will act indifferently, causing them to suspect loss of interest in them.

Plow

To dream of seeing people plowing denotes good fortune and affirms that you are on the road to success. If you dream that you are doing the plowing, splendid rewards for your ongoing efforts will come soon. To dream of plowing is a good omen for marriage, procreation, and beginning new ventures. But what is begun will take time to come to fruition.

Plum

To dream of a plum predicts advancement. To eat a plum hints that you may be using up resources too quickly.

Pneumonia

To dream of someone suffering with this disease suggests unexpressed communications that weaken you and cause much distress. To overcome this illness indicates you will discover a truth that allows you to get past a restriction.

Pocket

To dream of a large pocket denotes resourcefulness; a small one signifies someone who prefers to prepare in advance for a situation. To see a pocket filled with valued articles refers to skills you can draw upon when needed. To see a pocket filled

214

with junk or unpleasant objects suggests negative attitudes need to be plucked out.

Pocketbook

To dream that you find a pocketbook filled with money is an excellent omen for your immediate success. To find one that is empty denotes shattered hopes.

Poet

To dream of hearing a poet give a moving rendition signifies a skill at touching others' hearts. To write a poem suggests great intuition, insight, and sensitivity toward others.

Poison

To dream of seeing others poisoned denotes an illness generally brought about through a contagious disease. To dream that you are poisoned foretells news from a distance that is painful and disturbing to you. To dream that you are preparing to poison someone denotes many plans you believed would work will prove unsuccessful. To poison someone suggests you are taking advantage of someone and should not be doing so. To dream of poison in a specific food implies that this food reacts in your system very badly and should be avoided. To dream of poison in a bottle or container warns of a situation that should be avoided, lest serious consequences occur.

Poker

To dream of playing poker indicates a taste for taking risks. If you win, it suggests success in business ventures. To see an expressionless poker face indicates you should show more reserve with others.

Police

To dream that the police want to arrest you for a charge you know nothing about denotes that you will win a competition relating to business conditions. To feel that you are guilty of a charge denotes the conclusion of bad business.

Polishing

To dream that you are polishing articles that are rusty and ugly, and succeed in improving their appearance, implies that you will rise to great heights of power. If your efforts are without results, struggles and disappointment lie ahead.

Pond

To dream that you are in a boat upon clear water is a sign that joy will enter your life. If the pond is a little one, you should concentrate on the small things and carry them out well. These little things will lead to larger successes later. If the pond is a large one, your career will take a new turn that will further your prospects.

Pony

To see a pony signifies long life and a comfortable income. To see a child ride a pony denotes pleasant pursuits to come. If you are in uncertain circumstances, it hints that remaining optimistic is warranted.

Pool

To dream of playing a game of pool or billiards indicates you could make better use of leisure time. If, however, you are overworked in general, it denotes a need for relaxation and periods with no serious pursuits.

Poorhouse

To dream of entering a poorhouse denotes that you have friends who, in reality, only need you to further their own selfish ambitions in their efforts to be successful. Reexamine your friendships carefully.

Popcorn

To dream of popcorn implies many pleasant outbursts in social situations that provide fun and entertainment. To eat popcorn, but never feel full, implies you are trying to cope with a difficult situation that is emotionally unsatisfying.

Pope

To dream of the Roman Catholic Pope suggests either you or someone close to you is acting in an independent and even tyrannical manner. Though the other party deserves respect, it hints that you should challenge them more often and not allow yourself to be overcome by them.

Porcupine

To dream of seeing a porcupine foretells disagreements relating to business. For the unmarried to dream of a porcupine predicts a delicate affair relating to a sweetheart.

Portrait

To dream of admiring a beautiful portrait of someone you know denotes long life to that individual. To give or receive a portrait predicts that you will hear deceptive flattery from an associate with whom you work closely.

Potatoes

To dream of potatoes in general is a good omen. To dream that you are planting potatoes denotes that your ambitions will be achieved. To dig them is an excellent omen for success. Eat them, and you will achieve success.

Poultry

To dream of live poultry denotes valuable time wasted on silly pleasures. To dream of stuffed poultry predicts that your generous ways will bring you many friends who will stick by you while your money lasts.

Poverty

To dream of poverty is a warning to give excellent service in your career lest you lose your advantage. If you have attained wealth and prosperity, it warns you to be generous with your time and material goods, lest your old state befall you.

Prairie

To see a prairie in your dream denotes luxuries and a trouble-free life; also, that you are very popular. To dream that you are lost on one indicates that you may experience sadness and disappointments.

Prayer

To dream of saying your prayers denotes disagreements and trouble among friends. To dream of seeing others saying their prayers predicts happy events.

Preacher

To dream that you are a preacher, or are preaching, signifies that plans will fail to materialize. To dream of hearing a preacher preach signifies dissatisfaction caused by others who are blaming you for something.

Precipice

To dream of falling over a precipice denotes hostility, anger, and danger for the dreamer. To dream of being on the edge of a precipice relates to impending losses and disasters.

Predecessors

To dream of your predecessors, such as your grandfather or others, is a reminder of your immediate and long-term obligations. You should examine whether you are adequately fulfilling duties to yourself, to your loved ones, and to society.

Pregnancy

For a husband to dream that his wife is pregnant, and in reality she is pregnant, denotes a safe delivery, with no complications. For a woman to dream that she is pregnant implies that disagreements and misunderstanding will be her chief obstacle in life. For a virgin or unmarried woman to dream of being pregnant is a warning that she is considering a marriage that may prove disastrous, and that she should have second thoughts.

Preserves

To dream of a jar of jam or preserves hints that putting aside some present gains or funds will come in handy in the future.

President

To dream of the president of a country or a company foretells a major advancement in career.

Pretzel

To dream of a pretzel denotes an unpretentious and straight-forward personality. To eat a pretzel signifies an ability to appreciate the basic joys of life.

Priest

To dream that you are confessing to a priest implies humiliation caused by unfair publicity. For a young woman to dream that she is in love with a priest implies that she is placing her confidence in a liar.

Prison

To dream of a prison usually denotes misunderstandings with friends which will cause you stress. To dream of being in prison denotes troubles and disappointment to the dreamer.

Prize

To dream you receive a prize denotes achievement and honors due to persistent efforts.

Profanity

To dream of hearing profane language foretells dealing with unscrupulous people.

Promenade

To dream that you are promenading denotes that you will engage in a profitable business. To see others promenading means keen competition in business lies ahead.

Property

To dream of receiving property as a gift implies prosperity and ultimate wealth. To dream of losing property foretells that you will suffer financially from someone failing to follow your instructions.

Proposal

To dream of receiving a proposal of marriage indicates a successful partnership, whether it be in business or love. To hear a business proposal hints of success in that area, especially if there is an urgent tone to the proposal.

Prostitute

To dream of being in a prostitute's company denotes that you will be blamed for things you have done. To dream of being bothered by a prostitute denotes that you are very popular with the opposite sex, and that they think of you as their idol.

Prunes

To see or to eat prunes denotes joy. Dried prunes relate to

problems. To dream of them in winter means obstacles and difficulties, but only for a short duration.

Publishing

To dream you publish something is a signal to communicate as much as possible with others, in speech or in writing, as this will bring benefits. If you persist, you can get published, in time.

Puddings

To dream of seeing pudding being made denotes that you will profit from an unlikely investment. To dream that you are eating pudding means that troubles and disappointments lie ahead.

Pulpit

To dream that you are speaking from a pulpit, or that you are standing in a pulpit, denotes sorrows and discontentment due to poor business dealings and lack of opportunities.

Pulse

To dream that you feel someone's pulse denotes that your actions will be exposed and publicly criticized. To feel your own pulse is a sign that you are suffering from stress and need relaxation.

Pump

To dream that you are pumping clear water means that you will attain much joy and success. To dream of seeing others pumping water foretells that those who are less successful than you are jealous of the influence that you wield among your friends.

Pumpkin

To see a pumpkin in a dream foretells something will come to fruition for you in the fall.

Punishment

To dream of undergoing punishment denotes temporary success and wealth. To cause another to be punished indicates that you enjoy causing spiteful situations for others.

Puppies

To dream of puppies predicts you will enjoy many trusted friends. This is especially true if the puppies are healthy and cute. Should they be thin and sickly-looking, the reverse of the above would be the case.

Purchase

To dream of making a purchase denotes that you will forget or misplace something you will need badly; however, you will not necessarily lose it.

Purse

To dream of finding a purse containing money and other valuables foretells that you will receive money that you are really looking for.

Puzzle

To dream of a jigsaw puzzle implies that many details need to be worked out before something can be successful.

Puzzled

To see yourself or someone else puzzled in a dream signals a need to review a present situation. There is more to it than meets the eye.

Pyramid

To dream of climbing a pyramid denotes that you will take a long extended vacation that you've been looking forward to with pleasure. To dream of seeing a pyramid implies wealth and joy, and a possible raise in the near future.

Q

"And it shall come to pass afterward, that I will pour out my spirit upon all flesh; and your sons and your daughters shall prophesy, your old men shall dream dreams, your young men shall see visions."

JOEL 2:28

Quail

To dream of quails is considered a very favorable omen. To dream of killing them indicates selfishness shown by your friends. To dream of eating quail implies over-generosity, which should be controlled.

Quaint Scene

To see a quaint scene indicates harmony, traditional values, and goodwill. These are qualities that either exist in your life or are ones you long for. This dream may also reflect new acquaintances that you've wondered about.

Quaker

To dream of a Quaker suggests that the qualities of peacefulness and inner quietness would be valuable.

Quality

To see something of excellent quality in a dream is a signal that you should reach only for the best, and you will obtain it. If the quality of an item is especially poor, it warns you not to be taken in by a present prospect, nor to settle for something substandard.

Quarantine

To dream that you are held in quarantine warns of numerous spiteful actions taken by vicious people.

Quarrel

To dream of quarreling with a stranger denotes that you will shortly make a new acquaintance, one who will make you sorry you ever met. To quarrel with a friend implies that you will soon have a pleasant time with a friend. For lovers to dream of quarreling predicts that they will be more in love than before.

Quarry

To dream of falling into a quarry warns that you will have many problems due to your enemies. To dream of working in a quarry denotes that your success is only gained after much hard work and careful saving.

Quartet

To dream that you belong to or are singing in a quartet denotes that harmony and congenial surroundings will make life worthwhile.

Queen

To dream of a queen is a lucky omen. It speaks of success in recent investments. To dream of a queen who has lost her beauty denotes disappointments.

Question

To dream of asking a question denotes that your integrity is recognized, and that you will soon be promoted to a trusted position. For you to question another implies that deceitful friends are trying to hurt you.

Quiche

To dream of ordering a quiche in a restaurant suggests a rivalry, perhaps between a man and a woman. To prepare a quiche is an indication of a desire to do something special for another. If it is prepared successfully, you will please another greatly.

Quick

To see someone especially quick in movement is a signal that you need to move fast on something, lest you lose your advantage. To hear someone speak quickly suggests intelligence if the scene is positive, or nervousness if it is not.

Quicksand

To dream of sinking in quicksand denotes trouble and problems caused by liars. To see others in quicksand denotes that you will frustrate the plans of someone who is trying to hurt you. To see someone sink in quicksand anytime in a dream is a dire warning. To a businessman, it can warn that a new proposition will not hold ground and should be completely avoided. To someone in an unhappy relationship, it can suggest that the relationship will not improve, and that you should save yourself before it worsens. Any decision contemplated at this time should be made very conservatively.

Quiet

To dream of a scene that is especially quiet and tranquil predicts a period of great peace. However, if there is an unhappy or negative sense to the dream, it can suggest that being quiet or holding back on your part is detrimental at this time.

Quill

To see an old-fashioned quill pen suggests that information from your past, or from antiquity, will be helpful in a report or a communication of some sort.

Quilt

To dream of making a quilt indicates your work will be appreciated, and in time will be acknowledged as something special. To receive a beautiful quilt predicts that you will be honored for many talents and many years of work, if you continue on your present path.

Quinine

To dream of taking quinine means renewed energy to deal with your problems. To dream of giving it to others means dividends from hopeful prospects will be very small and will remain uncertain.

Quit

To see someone quit in anger warns that bad attitudes which may be building will lead to confrontation and consequences; however, a more conciliatory attitude would avert this. To quit calmly and with confidence suggests that it may be time to move on in your career.

Quoits

To dream of playing quoits foretells an ambition that is slow in realization. To see others play denotes that your success will depend much upon your power of concentration.

Quotation

To dream of hearing or reading a quotation of a famous or meaningful passage or line indicates you should seek wisdom from the words or writings of others.

R

"Sleep is often the only occasion in which man cannot silence his conscience; we forget what we knew in our dream."

ERICH FROMM, American psychoanalyst

Rabbits

To dream of rabbits is good. Conditions are sure to move along smoothly and bring good profits. To the lover, it denotes a proposal through a letter; accept it and happiness is yours. For a married woman to dream of these animals foretells an increase in the family.

Raccoon

To dream of a raccoon implies you are in a difficult period and must take whatever work or help from others you are offered.

Race

To dream that you are running a race and win foretells victory in business affairs; to lose a race implies others are interfering in your efforts.

Radar

To see a radar device or screen hints that your actions and attitudes are being watched by those in authority. A word to the wise is sufficient.

Radishes

To dream of radishes denotes that your ambition will be swiftly realized. To dream of eating them warns that you will suffer though someone's deceit. If you like radishes, to dream of them can signify a promise of abundance and fresh excitement in a new endeavor. If you dislike radishes, it can denote that bitterness and unpleasantness will surround a new endeavor.

Raffle

To dream of participating in a raffle suggests that some risk and effort should be given toward a worthwhile cause. To win a raffle indicates rewards will come for honest labor.

Raft

To dream of being adrift on a raft, but merry in spirit, suggests an adventurous vacation that will renew you. To be on a raft but feel stranded indicates that you have not sufficiently prepared yourself for life in career or love, and now feel the consequences. Yet, if action is taken, this can be changed.

Rage

To dream that you are in a terrible rage denotes that you will have quarrels with friends, which may end in bodily harm. To see others carrying on in this manner denotes that business is slowly declining. For an unmarried woman to dream of being in a rage implies that she is mistaken if she thinks her lover is faithful.

Rags

To see someone clothed in rags refers to the role you are assuming in life. If you are trying to "keep up with the Joneses," it implies that accepting less would be beneficial. If you are putting on airs regarding your position in life, rags suggest people see through it, and it demeans them. But, if you are struggling financially, the dream indicates the situation will not change quickly. To see rags destroyed, or thrown away, predicts affluence to come.

Railroad

To dream of a railroad generally refers to travels. If the road is clear, safe trips. To see an obstruction warns of unpleasant trips. In business, unfavorable conditions. To dream of walking on a railroad denotes worries and disappointments lie in the future.

Rain

To dream of being in a soft rain indicates good things to the dreamer. To dream of being in a terrible rainstorm warns of losses and irritations to those who are affluent, and good things to those who are poor.

Rainbow

To see a rainbow in your dream predicts good things for the

dreamer. A lull in business will turn to a more promising aspect. For sweethearts to dream of a rainbow denotes that their union will bring happiness and contentment.

Raincoat

To dream of a raincoat can refer to a tendency to cut yourself off from the emotions of others. Or, if surrounded by very emotional conditions, a raincoat suggests you have the strength to handle it.

Raisins

To dream of hungering for raisins or other sweets suggests a need to add some joy to your life. To dream of eating raisins denotes a realization of wealth and joy. Wealth, however, may come slowly; but it will come, nevertheless. To dream of eating raisins or other dried fruit always indicates joyful moments soon to come.

Rake

To dream of a rake or of raking leaves is a signal that leftovers from the past need to be cleared before progress can be made. To see someone raking happily suggests much will open up for you.

Ram

To dream of being bucked by a ram denotes that you will be reprimanded by one for whom you failed to perform requested duties.

Ramp

To see a ramp that makes it possible to move from a difficult spot predicts a solution to a problem.

Rape

To dream that a person you know has been raped denotes that you will hear of some scandal surrounding dear friends. For an unmarried woman to dream that she has been raped implies that she will hear damaging news relating to the one she loves.

Raspberries

To dream of raspberries in season is a good omen. To a businessman it predicts success due to his own determination and strict attention to business. For an unmarried woman to dream of raspberries means that her lover will be industrious and a good provider.

Rats

To dream of rats is a bad sign of loss by theft. To hear them gnawing is unusually bad. When a woman who has a lover dreams of rats, it is a warning for caution in order to protect her honor. To see a rat often denotes something that is gnawing at you, whether it be a temptation or something causing anxiety. Solutions are found by staying calm and adhering to a single course of action.

Raven

To dream of ravens relates to unhappy conditions in business

234

affairs. To kill them denotes a quarrel due to your defiance and resistance.

Razor

To dream of sharpening a razor for the sole purpose of fighting with another means conflicts that may prove disastrous. To dream of cutting yourself means you will have enemies to deal with.

Reading

To dream of reading the Bible signifies inner strength you can draw on. To read an official document denotes upcoming details that will be important to understand. To read works of science or art denotes aptitude in these fields. To read a sad letter foretells sorrowful news.

Reapers

To dream of seeing reapers in the field busily harvesting an abundant crop implies prosperity and great joy. To dream of seeing them idle denotes that your efforts in a current project will yield little success for you at the time, but your fortunes may change later on.

Rebel

To see someone as a rebel who succeeds hints that you are taking regulations too seriously. However, if the rebel meets great trouble and failure in the dream, it suggests rebellious attitudes and actions are inappropriate at this time and would only bring trouble.

Reception

To dream of attending a classy reception denotes others will receive your ideas and work with open arms. But if you are treated badly or denied entrance, it predicts those around you will be negative toward your work, whether or not this is deserved.

Record Player

To see a record player signifies a trip through memory lane, whether it be a pleasant one or not. To hear beautiful music played on a record player denotes spiritual growth.

Reference Material

To dream of looking up references in a library, or in the back of a book, is a sign that you should compare your own ideas and work with others before proceeding further, which will help your progress.

Reflection

To see a reflection in a mirror indicates you should take a closer look at yourself from the inside out. To see a reflection in water, or on a shiny surface, indicates you are kidding yourself about something.

Refrigerator

To dream of a refrigerator denotes that you will hurt a friend's feelings at a party by acting selfishly. Rude comments will be made about your behavior and your reputation may suffer.

236

Regatta

To see many beautiful sailing ships on a clear lake predicts work that requires interaction with many in the community and brings much happiness. It suggests an ability to put others at ease.

Reindeer

To dream of reindeer denotes many true and devoted friends. To drive one denotes a gain in businesss through the prestige of people not connected with the business.

Relatives (Alive)

When you dream of another person, whether a relative, friend, or stranger, most often the characteristics of that person are a mirror for those you are currently dealing with. However, if you are close to a relative or friend, and dream of them, it may hint at their real state of mind or emotion. The dream may tell you something important that they are too shy or afraid to share with you directly.

Relatives (Deceased)

To dream of a deceased loved one is a sign of great importance. If the dream discusses a matter important to you now, it denotes advice as though coming directly from the loved one. If the deceased person is in an unhappy state, you are advised to pray for the loved one. If the deceased person is giving reassurance, it portends the end of a current problem. Or, reassurance by the loved one can indicate that all is well in their new, non-earthly home; you should cease worrying about your deceased loved one and get on with your life.

Relics

To dream of relics is a warning to be careful with some household valuable. To dream of receiving a relic denotes that you will break or spoil something that you value highly.

Rent

To dream of paying rent indicates you have the ability to sustain yourself. To demand rent suggests someone in your life is not pulling their weight.

Reptiles

To dream of reptiles that appear harmless while you watch their graceful movements denotes the settlement of money that you had thought was as good as lost. To dream of seeing them viciously wanting to attack you implies that enemies will renew their bitterness toward you. To dream of killing reptiles foretells that you will overcome great obstacles. To handle them without harm portends that the bitterness of friends will be replaced by pleasure and happiness.

Rescue

To dream of rescuing someone signifies you have taken a giant step in maturity and are able to use talents to assist others. To be rescued suggests help will be available when you need it.

Resignation

To dream that you have resigned your position predicts that an advantageous change is in store for you shortly.

Revenge

To dream of avenging yourself denotes an insensitive nature on your part. This tendency will be the cause of losing many good friends.

Revolver

To handle a revolver in your dream is not good. It relates to quarrels and conflict. You should cultivate more self-control. For an unmarried woman to dream of this firearm denotes an interference with someone she loves.

Rheumatism

To dream of this affliction is a warning to let go of anger and guilt and to get on with using your talents, lest your energies be slowly drained.

Rhinoceros

To dream of a rhinoceros suggests that you are strong and persistent, which serves you well; but perhaps you are also a little stubborn, which does not.

Rhubarb

To dream of this vegetable denotes that you are a good-natured person; many people enjoy being in your company to listen to your philosophy. To dream of eating rhubarb means that present plans will end favorably.

Ribbon

To see a display of ribbon in your dreams denotes a happy and good-natured disposition, and that you can put aside your problems when you choose to do so. For an unmarried woman to dream of ribbons denotes that her sweetheart is only having a good time; but he'll soon settle down.

Ribs

If a man dreams that his upper ribs are broken, it warns him that fighting and dissension are about to erupt in an important relationship. If a man dreams that his lower ribs are broken, it implies that health problems may be building up; he is advised to note symptoms and seek medical advice. However, if he dreams that his ribs have grown stronger and longer than normal, it is an indication of sexual prowess.

Rice

To dream of eating rice signifies domestic bliss and business success. To see a quantity of rice implies prosperity in all work aspects and many true friends.

Riches

To dream that you are rich denotes that your aggressive and firm nature will bring you what you justly deserve.

Riding

To dream of riding on a bus denotes that you are attempting to make a decision, which is likely related to a change in a work situation. If you reach your destination, the change will be made successfully. To dream of riding a swift animal, such as a horse, signifies much pleasure in the senses, which may need to be balanced or kept under control. If you are riding a slow beast such as an ox, it suggests that you need to partici- pate more in life's pleasures.

Ringing

To dream of hearing bells ring indicates that important news will soon reach you. If the mood of the dream is somber and dreary, making you feel uncomfortable or wary, the news is unwelcome. If the mood is pleasant and makes you feel good, the news will be welcome.

Rings

To dream of seeing rings on your fingers implies new plans which will generally turn out well. To see rings sticking in the ground with only the settings visible, and then you pluck them out, denotes disappointments relating to business. For an unmarried woman to receive a ring means that an old love affair will be revived and end in marriage.

Riot

To see a riot in progress means disappointments. To dream of seeing someone you know killed in a riot predicts poor con- ditions in business.

Rival

To dream of having differences with a rival denotes that you are weak, indecisive, and afraid to assert your rights. To suc- ceed in removing your rival means that you are a splendid leader and that you should seek a leadership position.

River

To dream of a clear and tranquil river is a lucky sign, particularly for people in a professional calling. To dream of a wavy, rising river means jealousy and dissatisfaction. To see a river overflow its banks, and the water is clear, denotes meeting a person of distinction. If the water is muddy, it foretells that lack of interest caused by indiscreet actions of others must be settled.

Road

To dream of following a straight and easy road denotes joy and prosperity. To be on a road that winds and is hard to follow denotes changes that will be unfavorable.

Robin

To see a robin sing is an indication that consistent efforts will lead to a secure and happy life.

Rocks

To find yourself climbing on rocks and succeed in reaching the top denotes joy and happiness. To dream that you fail to reach the top denotes disappointment and obstacles.

Roof

To dream of being on a roof indicates success. If you have difficulty in getting down, it denotes that your success is of an uncertain nature. To dream of seeing others on a roof who are unable to get down implies petty irritations.

Roosters

To dream of a rooster is a happy omen; it relates to great success. But the success may have a tendency to make you conceited and unbearable in your actions, and you may, therefore, lose the respect of others.

Roots

To dream of the roots of a tree or other large vegetation means that you will connect to some well established group or organization, either in business or in extracurricular activities. If the roots belong to a small plant or shrub, it is a signal to examine whether the activities in your life are sufficiently nurturing.

Ropes

To dream of climbing a rope, and to succeed in reaching the desired spot, means that you will overcome your enemies. To fail in climbing the rope successfully foretells of interferences from someone you have no choice in dealing with. To dream of walking a rope denotes that you will succeed in some investment. To see others walking a rope means acquisitions through the kind assistance of friends. To dream of jumping rope predicts that you are well liked and respected by those who are your friends.

Rosemary

To dream you smell the herb rosemary denotes some person or some activity from your past is about to come back into your life again.

Roses

To dream of seeing beautiful roses in season denotes that success is heading your way; it also speaks of happy events. For an unmarried woman to dream of gathering roses denotes an early proposal from her ideal man.

Rotten

To dream of rotten food hints that you react badly to certain foods, which can lead to illness. It may also mean that some involvement or activity is not good for you and is about to become unpleasant. To dream of rotted wood, or parts of a home, warns that issues which have been long-neglected, unless corrected, will lead to things falling apart.

Rowing

To dream that you are rowing in a boat with others denotes that you will enjoy the pleasure of happy and knowledgeable associates. Should the boat you are rowing capsize, you may face monetary difficulties due to slow business. If you win a boat race, honors will be yours. If you lose, you will lose your loved one to a rival.

Rubbing

To dream of rubbing something that is dusty and bringing it to a shiny glow indicates success with areas or items that others do not care for. To have your back or shoulders rubbed in a dream suggests solace and consolation will be yours.

Ruins

To dream of a ruin implies an unexpected acquisition or fortune. To dream of being among ruins means discoveries that will lead to success. To dream of ancient ruins refers to extensive travels in foreign lands.

Running

To dream of running fast is an excellent omen; your plans will materialize quickly. To stumble or fall means disappointment. If running after an enemy, victory; great profit if you catch the enemy. To run naked signifies trust violated by relatives. For a sick person to dream of running indicates disaster to the dreamer. For a woman to dream of running nude foretells her dishonor and loss of friends.

Rupture

To see anything rupturing warns that too much is demanded of something or someone, which will lead to an unpleasant and sudden ending; but if action is taken quickly, this can be averted.

S

"In dreams we see ourselves naked and acting our real characters, even more clearly than we see others awake."

HENRY DAVID THOREAU, American writer

Saddle

To see a saddle without a horse suggests loss of power in career or lack of a mate, but this can be temporary. To place a saddle on a horse indicates strong energies and empowerment.

Safe

To dream of a safe denotes that your business will prosper without serious problems. To dream of opening or working the combination of a safe denotes a disappointment relating to business matters that you initially believed to be a good investment.

Sailing

To dream that you are out sailing on calm waters means excellent success in whatever is attempted. To be on wavy, murky water predicts unpleasant occurrences that will deplete your energies.

Sailor

To dream of seafarers predicts unpleasant and exciting trips by water. For an unmarried woman to dream of a sailor as her suitor denotes struggles due to her overanxious desire for admiration.

Salad

To eat salad in your dream denotes that you will be bored by disagreeable people. For an unmarried woman to dream of making salad denotes that she should insist on an early marriage because her lover is unpredictable and fickle.

Salary

To dream of a raise in salary is a signal that your good work is gaining attention and will reap rewards. To hear news of a lowering of salary denotes changes in responsibilities, which you will not enjoy.

Sale

To buy something on sale that is a great bargain predicts a valuable opportunity that you will not expect, and it will be very favorable. To see items on sale suggests that something for which you hoped to see progress will not occur. To seek out a sale suggests you could make better use of assets and finances. If you tend to overwork, it also hints that you would like and should receive more material reward for what you do.

Salmon

To dream of salmon often refers to troubles in the family. To eat salmon predicts arguments with neighbors.

Salt

To dream of salt foretells of conflicts with close associates. To dream of spilling salt means enemies will openly accuse you of a wrongdoing. To an unmarried woman, dreaming of salt means lovers' quarrels due to jealousy on her part, because the sweetheart is talking about women she dislikes. Don't pay attention to what is said, and there will be no argument.

Sand

To dream of small grains of sand, especially among other objects, signifies annoyances.

Sandwich

To dream you eat sandwiches indicates moderate financial achievement. If you eat with gusto, it is more than you had before.

Sapphire

To dream of this gem denotes a need for patience and faithful support of another.

Sardines

To dream of these small fish speaks of abundance that can be yours if you treat others well.

Sash

For a young and unmarried woman to dream of wearing a long sash denotes that her sweetheart is faithful but conceals his affections for an obvious reason.

Satan

To see some form of a satanic figure in your dreams relates to business plans that may prove futile. To dream that you are fleeing from the devil denotes that you will conquer your enemies and turn them into your best friends. To dream of being punished by Satan is a warning against believing flatterers who are trying to win your confidence.

Sausage

To dream of making sausages is a warning of excessive sexual pleasure. To eat sausages indicates love intrigues.

Saw

Dreaming of saws, in general, is good. To dream that you are working with a saw predicts activity and energy that will most certainly bring about a comfortable life. To dream of seeing others working with a saw foretells of gains that were thought to be impossible.

Scabs

To dream of scabs on the body implies bitterness about the past. It is advisable to forgive and forget.

Scaffold

To dream of a scaffold denotes disappointments that will greatly hurt your dignity. To examine a scaffold implies deceit from those you have always trusted.

Scalding

To dream of scalding yourself with hot water denotes self-destructive behavior, especially of misdirected emotions. To see another scalded is a warning that your words may have a stronger negative effect than you are aware; more sensitivity on your part is required.

Scales

To dream that you are weighing yourself on a scale denotes an increase in your financial situation, and that pending investments will bring flattering results. To see others weighing themselves indicates that you lack decision-making ability and depend too much on others' opinions.

Scalp

To see a diseased scalp is a dire warning that your thinking and present attitudes, if continued, will bring great trouble into your life. You are advised to retain high standards. To be scalped predicts you will lose in some competitive endeavor, or warns that your thinking is off-base.

Scandal

To dream of being involved in a scandal is a warning to keep all dealings with others strictly decent and aboveboard, lest scandal unwittingly befall you. To see others involved warns that situations around you could lead to trouble.

Scar

To see scars on legs suggests many challenges. Scars on the arms indicate that your own aggressive attitudes may bring on problems. Scars on the face speak of negative attitudes that you are cautioned to change.

School

To dream that you are young and attending school indicates distinction in some mental line. To dream of visiting a school-house where you once attended implies petty annoyances related to present business.

Schooner

To see this ship in a dream suggests that you must carry heavy burdens and responsibilities with little appreciation. Your station in life will not yet change.

Scissors

To dream of scissors means trouble. For the married, it tells of jealousy and suspicion; to sweethearts, quarrels and accusations, and a love that won't run smoothly.

Scold

To dream of scolding another suggests those under your care are not living up to the best they can. To be scolded says the same for you. If the scene is exaggerated, it suggests you are too harsh in your criticisms of others, and though your words are warranted, you should add understanding and tact.

Scorpions

To dream of scorpions signifies you will meet slander from an unexpected source, and it will be painful.

Scratch

To dream that you have a bleeding scratch on you denotes that enemies are trying to destroy your property; if the scratch does not bleed, their plans will fail and you will enjoy peace and prosperity.

Screech Owl

To dream of hearing the sounds of this owl implies bereavement, usually the death of a near relative.

Scrubbing

To dream of scrubbing an item indicates the need to start fresh with something.

Sculptor

To dream of a sculptor means a change in your profession, generally to one of great importance that will command more respect.

Scythe

To dream of this implement denotes that some unforeseen circumstances will prevent you from performing your duties properly. To dream of one that is old and worn out means troubles with friends due to your bluntness.

Sea

To dream of the sea denotes pleasant and happy travels. For an unmarried woman to dream that she is on a calm sea with her lover denotes marital happiness. To dream of hearing the roaring of the sea in a storm foretells of a lonely life due to your reserved and self-centered tendencies.

Seal

To dream of seals denotes very extravagant tastes that will be the cause of great hardship later in life. It is a warning that your extravagance is abnormal, and that you should control it to avoid problems in the future.

Sea Serpent

To dream of a sea serpent hints that scary episodes from the past can come back to haunt you, unless you receive professional help. However, if the sea creature is amusing and endearing, it indicates creative ideas that can come to you in times of quiet.

Seashore

To dream of standing on the seashore, or of watching the majesty of the ocean, is an assurance of much help and protection. To dream of watching the tide come in or out denotes a need for patience, because the timing of something is not quite right. To see someone in a dream pulled by a current beneath the surface of the water suggests that private matters are strongly affecting you and could destroy what you have built up.

Seasickness

To dream of seasickness indicates you are in emotional situations that are over your head, which are best avoided or ended.

Seat

To dream of falling off a seat forewarns that you will meet a challenge in the work place that can bring a career setback. If you hold a position of authority or high office, someone will attempt to usurp your position.

Sect

To dream of a traditional religious sect denotes you seek community with others of like mind. To dream of a strange sect warns not to get involved with a group of people.

Security Guard

To dream of calling upon the services of a watchman in whom you have confidence suggests that a concern you have will soon be put to rest. To see a watchman sleeping on the job warns you to be vigilant in your responsibility, lest adverse effects befall you.

Seducer

For an unmarried woman to dream of being seduced denotes

that she is too sentimental and impressionable. The dreamer should cultivate more strength of character and set goals in life. Should a man dream of betraying a woman in this manner implies that false accusations will be directed against him that will humiliate him.

Seizure

To dream of being afflicted with seizures is an indication of an illness that will make you unable to perform your duties. To dream of seeing others suffering from seizures is a sign of deceit among your fellow workers.

Sell

To sell something at a loss indicates regret; what is gone will cause you sorrow. To dream that something is sold is a sign of an upcoming ending. You are advised to let go gracefully of whatever exits your life. To sell something at a profit portends a better situation ahead.

Serenade

To dream of hearing a serenade denotes that you will receive pleasant and delightful distant news. To help to serenade someone means splendid things are in store for you. Serenades often suggest a love interest, but the outcome is uncertain.

Seriousness

To see someone behave in a serious manner is an invitation to one who has been flighty to become more serious.

Serpents

To dream of serpents generally denotes enemies and ingratitude from friends. To see them curl, twist, and crawl denotes hatred and illness. To kill them means victories over enemies. If you capture one, you'll succeed in destroying jealousy.

Servant

To dream of discharging a servant implies losses and regretful occurrences. To dream of quarreling with a servant denotes that you are too friendly with your servants; show more dignity and make them look up to you.

Sewing

To dream of sewing and altering denotes disappointment in an anticipated event. To dream of sewing something brand new means that joy and contentment will soon be yours.

Sewing Machine

To see a sewing machine implies that something needs to be secured. To use one suggests you need to adopt an attitude of service.

Shadow

To see shadows that appear sinister suggests you fear your own motives and inclinations, which need to be examined. To see someone or something cast a long shadow denotes you will encounter someone or something of importance.

Shame

To dream of someone who feels shame indicates feelings of guilt that need to be let go of.

Shampoo

To dream of seeing someone being shampooed denotes that you will be requested to perform a duty that you'll consider to be undignified. To dream of having your own hair shampooed denotes that you must be more secretive, or you will arouse suspicion in others.

Shamrock

To dream of a shamrock denotes good fortune that comes from your skills in communication and your ability to make people feel good.

Shark

To dream of a mean-looking shark warns that someone has a grudge against you and seeks to hurt you. Or, if you are holding a grudge, it suggests you will do damage if you act on it.

Shaving

To dream of being shaved closely denotes that a friend will help you by paying a loan that is due. To dream of shaving yourself predicts that you will incur a debt innocently, or perhaps overdraw your bank account.

Shawl

To see a beautiful shawl indicates grace and dignity.

Shearing

To dream of shearing sheep signifies a favorable business exchange, but one for which steady application of work will be required.

Sheep (see Lamb)

To dream of seeing a flock of sheep denotes good luck to the dreamer. To see them thin and sick-looking denotes debts brought about through poor financing. To dream of cutting their wool signifies rewarded efforts.

Shell

To dream of a seashell indicates that you have intuition at your disposal.

Shelter

To dream of seeking shelter from rain relates to secret problems. To dream of seeking shelter from a storm denotes that the optimism you now hold for your present plans will turn into despair.

Sheriff

To dream that you succeed in hiding from a sheriff denotes that you are carrying on with illegitimate plans, which will be profitable for a short time. To dream of being apprehended by a sheriff implies that present difficulties will result in more joyful times ahead.

Ship

To dream of seeing a ship in perfect condition is a good sign.

To dream of a ship in great distress in stormy waters denotes troubles in conducting your business, or that a secret about you will be revealed, which will ruin your reputation forever.

Shipwreck

To dream of a shipwreck, in general, is a very bad omen. It is a warning that unexpected disaster is imminent in the area of life in which you most avoid responsibility. If you have not held to good health habits, your health is at risk. If you have not fortified your career, a job can be lost. If you have not given time and attention to loved ones, those dear to you may abandon you. But if the shipwreck is threatening but has not yet occurred, it is a sign that the trouble can be avoided if you take action. To see others shipwrecked means distress over someone's wrongdoings. To dream of being shipwrecked yourself denotes danger, or loss of your reputation.

Shirt

To dream of taking off your shirt predicts a separation from a loved one, generally due to your inconsiderate actions. To see your shirt torn in your dream relates to pleasant surprises. To lose it signifies troubles in business or affairs of the heart. To dream of a soiled shirt predicts that you are overly stressed, and that you need to take a vacation.

Shoes

To dream of shoes that are badly worn or worn down denotes that you lack tact and are too blunt and outspoken; consequently, you make enemies. To dream of having shoes shined means prosperity and happy events. To see your shoes untied portends disagreements in friendship. New shoes mean good news and hopes to be realized. For a young woman to dream that a gentleman removed her shoes denotes that the dreamer must be cautious, for her lover may make sexual overtures toward her.

Shooting
To dream that you are shooting denotes misunderstandings between friends. To hear shooting means disagreements in your marriage. To sweethearts, shooting denotes quarrels of a temporary nature that will be resolved in the near future.

Shoplifting
To see someone steal in public indicates dishonest circum-stances that are best avoided. To see yourself steal warns that lowering your standards will bring you harm.

Shopping
To dream of going shopping signifies success in life. To shop for a specific item foretells new directions.

Shoulders
To dream of broad, muscular shoulders indicates new strength and confidence unfolding. Thereafter, you are likely to take on new responsibilities and ventures that were always desired, but hitherto out of reach. However, if the shoulders are stooped and weak, this denotes that you have not lived up to your own standards; you are advised to reexamine your life.

Shovel

To see a shovel signifies a tool or technique you need to incorporate. To use a shovel suggests you are overdoing something.

Shower

To dream of a rain shower is a sign of an upcoming respite to one who has been overburdened. Or, it can indicate the attainment of a goal to one who had cherished a dream but had been unable to fulfill it. To dream of taking a shower for cleansing denotes that you will start fresh because a new cycle in life is about to begin; it is a signal to prepare to take a new direction.

Showing Off

To see someone showing off is an indication that you feel too important, or you are around someone who has a swelled head.

Shroud

To dream of a shroud predicts unhappiness and a tendency to illness, from which business may suffer. To dream of seeing a shroud removed portends arguments and disagreements from a source you least expect.

Sickness

To dream that you are sick denotes sadness and sorrow. To

nurse the sick indicates joy, profit, and happiness. To see a member of your family sick predicts an unexpected pleasure that will end in sadness.

Sieve

To dream of a sieve implies that you need to refine something, or to lighten up.

Sign

To see a prominent sign in a dream hints that you need to pay attention to how circumstances are shaping up around you, because change is inevitable.

Silk

To dream of silk, in any form, is a happy sign; your ambition will be achieved, and happiness will replace any present conflict. To dream of silk also means that you possess great pride in your work.

Silkworm

To dream of a silkworm implies that you are thinking about a new investment that will prove very successful. To see silkworms shedding their cocoons denotes success after you experience many obstacles.

Silver

To dream of silver money implies irritations relating to meeting obligations.

Silverware

To dream of silverware implies that the dreamer is too materialistic and takes little interest in the spiritual. Material pleasures seem to be very important. If you dream of silverware being lost or stolen, it would be advisable to examine the circumstances of loved ones to ensure that none are being led astray. To polish silverware happily in a dream predicts an event that will bring joy.

Singing

To dream that you are singing denotes that your happy moments will turn to sorrow. To the unmarried, singing indicates that suspicion and jealousy may soon arise and destroy their happy dreams. To hear others sing portends happy news and pleasant moments spent with cheerful friends.

Skating

To dream that you are skating denotes that you are about to make a change you will regret; think twice before you act. To dream of seeing skating denotes humiliation from those who are jealous of your position and will gossip about you.

Skeleton

To dream of seeing a skeleton approaching you foretells sad and shocking news. To dream of seeing a motionless skeleton implies enemies undermining your efforts.

Skull

To dream of skulls is a sign of family troubles and a general reminder of one another's shortcomings. To the unmarried, skulls indicate quarrels due to fickle and changeable personalities. To dream of a skull of someone you know means injured pride.

Skunk

To see a skunk spray you warns that others will betray you.

Sky

If you are about to embark on a marriage or a new relationship, to dream of a clear, blue sky denotes a happy outcome. If you are about to begin a new project or business dealing, it predicts much success. To dream of flying upward or ascending into the sky signifies an increase in honor and prestige, while a cloudy or dreary sky is a forecast of disappointment. A murky and dark sky warns of trouble ahead.

Slaughtering

To dream of animals or people being slaughtered or killed is an indication of great tension and strong emotions that seek expression. You will find peace in speaking to others about what you feel deeply.

Slave

To see a mistreated slave warns of another person taking advantage of you. To see a slave accepting his lot, or to be a slave, denotes work under another's direction that will be demanding, but also may be beneficial in the long term.

Sled

To dream of child's sled signifies a pleasant illusion that will do no harm, but the projected hope will not manifest. To ride an Olympic bobsled in a dream denotes a need for much assertion and team work in order to see something through.

Sleep

To dream of seeing others sleeping denotes that you will succeed in accomplishing your objective. To sleep with an ugly person implies sickness and discontent. For a young woman to dream of sleeping with a handsome man indicates troubles, irritations, and possible loss of something she loves. To sleep with a woman, if married, means troubles to your wife or family; if single, it means danger of deceptions, or that you will believe the lies told to you by a woman who wants you as her lover. To dream of being discovered with another denotes disappointment relating to money matters. To see someone napping in a dream signifies a need for rest to one who is overworked; or, to see someone napping may indicate a need to exert yourself to one who has not been working much. To dream of walking in your sleep indicates confusion in your life; a period of reflection is recommended.

Slender

To dream of wanting to be slender is an encouragement to reach for the best for yourself, physically and otherwise. To be slender in a dream, when in reality you are not, foretells much progress and accomplishment to come. To dream of someone who is too slender indicates a need to be loved, or that someone around you desperately needs attention.

Sliding

To dream of sliding down a deep slope denotes that you are too gullible, and may suffer a financial loss by placing too much confidence in a business venture. To slide, in general, implies disappointments. For lovers, differences over trivial matters are in store.

Slip

To dream that you slip and fall suggests that bad habits or uncontrolled outbursts will cause you to lose the respect of those around you.

Slippers

To receive a pair of slippers that is comfortable and good-looking is a signal of happiness at home.

Sloppy

To see yourself in a sloppy condition is an indication that either your attitudes or you physical habits need upgrading.

Smirk

To see someone smirk denotes others are not accepting what you say at face value, even if you communicate truthfully.

Smog

To see smog in a dream hints that anxieties and bad attitudes clouding your judgment and peace of mind need to be dealt with.

Smoke

To dream of being in, or suffering from, smoke denotes injury through the schemes of false friends. To see smoke means false glory.

Smother

To see something smothered in a dream signifies you are attempting to exert too much influence on something or someone, and you need to back off. If you are being smothered, this warns you to set limits for another not to trespass.

Snail

To see a snail crawl in your dream denotes an honorable responsibility. To see a snail with long horns means infidelity, adultery, and fondness for vulgarity. To step on a snail indicates you will meet people you wish you had not.

Snakes

To dream of snakes, as a rule, implies misfortune or immorality in some form or other. To dream that a snake bites you signifies a quarrel with a friend or relative. If a snake winds around you, and you are unable to conquer it, this tells of an enemy that will deeply anger you. To dream of being surrounded by these reptiles, and that you succeed in killing one out of many, signifies that someone will cheat you in money matters. To succeed in killing every snake around you predicts that you will have great power over your enemies. To walk over snakes without trying to kill them denotes that you are wearing out your nerves by useless worrying and fear. To dream that they bite you means that you will do something illegal or immoral through your enemies. To dream of handling snakes, if they seem playful and harmless, implies that you are inventing a plan to deceive those who oppose you. To step on snakes without being bitten denotes that you will be bored by those you thought were interesting.

Sneakers

To see a new pair of sneakers predicts a comfortable new life and lifestyle soon to be yours. To see an old pair of sneakers ready to fall apart suggests the time has come to move along in a job or relationship.

Sneeze

To dream of sneezing denotes the need to speak sharply and clearly to someone who has been aggravating you.

Sniper

To dream of a sniper stalking his prey suggests someone around you is two-faced and not a true friend. It is a warning not to mistake smiles for sincerity.

Snow

To dream that you are in a snowstorm denotes disappointment regarding a pleasure that you had been looking forward to with great enthusiasm. To dream of seeing dirty snow predicts that your pride will suffer and that you will acknowledge those you once thought were beneath you. To dream of being snowbound means that many obstacles and hard work lie ahead. To see a few inches of beautiful snow on the ground denotes joy and pleasure. To eat snow or to taste it means good health will be yours. To dream of seeing distinct snowflakes indicates you have unique, special talents that need to be identified, developed, and used; this will bring you much success and joy. To see many snowflakes denotes you will work with and have the companionship of many talented people.

Soap

To dream of soap denotes a need to communicate something you have been holding back, and also that you need to let go of the past.

Soap Opera

To dream you are in or observing a soap opera suggests that something in your life is being exaggerated, or that you or others are acting in a melodramatic fashion.

Social Climber

To see a social climber in a dream suggests you are putting on airs and not acting true to yourself and your true place in life.

Socks

To see brightly colored socks suggests you are making an impact with others. To see socks that are worn or have holes in them suggests you are losing your vibrancy; you need to regroup.

Soda

To dream of purchasing or consuming a soft drink indicates a need to lighten up and be more a part of life. If your attitude has been harsh, it hints at a need to soften it.

Solar House

To see a solar house denotes laudable self-sufficiency.

Soldiers

To dream that you are a soldier means that your ambition will be achieved. To see a wounded soldier denotes that the distressing condition of others has aroused your sympathy and will cause you to fight against them despite your better judgment. To see soldiers marching means a promotion for you. For an unmarried woman to dream of a soldier is a warning to resist immoral propositions. To dream of armed soldiers is a good sign that you have few fears. To see soldiers come in arms against you signifies that you have to do battle over something in order to achieve your aims.

Somersault

To dream of turning somersaults indicates unusual skills that will bring fame and good fortune.

Son

For a father or mother to dream of their son looking healthy, or anything that is favorable about him, denotes that he will make his mark in the world and gain great honor for his outstanding qualities. To dream of one's son in pain refers to grief, loss, and sorrow.

Song

To dream of singing a song beautifully denotes opportunities to use your talents. To hear a song sung hints that divine providence guides your fate.

Soprano

To hear a soprano sing suggests your talents are needed, most likely for a specific, upcoming project. Giving of yourself freely will bring glory.

Sorrow

To dream of feeling much sorrow indicates that healing of a past difficult situation has begun.

Sorting

To dream of sorting beautiful items suggests you have choices to make, and none will lead you into paths you will regret. To sort soiled or ugly things warns that choices being considered will lead to no good. If the items are mixed, it indicates the need to be careful in decision-making at this time.

Soup

To dream of eating soup foretells comfort and happiness. To see others eating it means few obstacles in your attempts.

Sour

To see a sour expression on a face warns that you attitude is becoming negative and needs your attention.

Sowing

To dream of seeing others sowing indicates an advancement in business matters. To dream of yourself sowing denotes hopes to be realized.

Spacecraft

To dream of a spacecraft implies unusual ideas that may be ahead of their time, but which are worth pursuing patiently. To ride in a spaceship implies you may feel cut off from others or that you are acting in a far-out manner.

Spark Plugs

If you dream your car needs spark plugs, check it out. If the car is fine, it may suggest you are missing an important connection, either in a relationship or in thinking, which is important to your future.

Sparrow

To dream of sparrows denotes that neighbors are jealous of your possessions or begrudge your success.

Speech

To dream of delivering a speech predicts success in influencing others. To hear a favorable speech suggests you can learn from another.

Spell

To see a spell cast in a dream implies you are being unduly influenced by another. Be sure decisions you make are truly your own.

Sphinx

To see this Egyptian creature, with a lion's body and a human head, indicates success through unusual creativity or ideas. These will bring wisdom and light to many.

Spice Rack

To see a rack with spices hints that you need to spice up your life. Seek to add new activities or ideas. Or, spices can denote that you already possess the talent to bring excitement to the lives of others, and you simply need to do so.

Spider

To see spiders in your dreams denotes that thrifty and conscientious tendencies will be the key to acquiring a large fortune. To dream of killing one signifies quarrels and hatred. For a young woman to dream of having a pet spider predicts that she will marry a professional man.

Spill

To see a spill in a dream denotes careless words or actions that will cause grief or disgrace.

Spinster

To dream of an unhappy spinster suggests opportunities can be lost unless you give freely of yourself. To dream of a serene spinster suggests that a period of being alone may befall you, but it will not last.

Spirit

To dream that you see a spirit or ghost before you, dressed in white and surrounded by light and beauty, signifies much soul progress, and denotes a spiritual blessing. If the spirit is ugly, fearful, or misshapen, you are warned to examine your habits, lest a bad habit or turn of life lead you astray and bring painful consequences.

Spitting
To dream of seeing someone spitting warns you of poor communications.

Splash
To see a great splash is a signal that a highly emotional situation can affect your life, even though you are not directly involved. Stay calm and let it pass.

Splinter
To dream of having a splinter in your body denotes that you will be annoyed by friends.

Split
To see something split in two warns that an estrangement can occur in a relationship unless you take care. To see pants split while being worn hints at the need to eat reasonably.

Sponge
To see a sponge that is full and soaked with clear water signifies that you are in a period where learning of any kind will greatly benefit you. Diligently pursue what interests you, for

it will bring great rewards. A full sponge can denote a satisfying emotional life. To dream of a dry sponge hints that you are emotionally hungry and need to seek out the companionship of a mate or friends.

Spoons

To dream of a spoon indicates marital happiness and contentment. To dream that you are stealing a spoon denotes that your company manners do not correspond with your at-home manners.

Sport

To see a competitive sport played warns that a situation will be challenging. To see a team win a sport indicates you will succeed by cooperating with others. To put in a lot of practice for an individual sport means that perfecting a talent would benefit you.

Spotlight

To see a spotlight shining in a dream suggests something you do will come to the attention of others. Make sure it is positive.

Spring (Water)

To dream of a spring of shining, beautiful, gushing water signifies much inner strength that will benefit you and others greatly. If the spring is dried up or carries muddy, unpleasant water, you are warned to let go of hatreds, ill will, and malice toward others, lest the same befall you.

Spurs (On Boots)

To see a rider's spurs suggests that you either need to get going with something you have been lax with, or that others will soon urge you to get going. Do so.

Spy

To see a spy scene in a dream implies that others are curious about you and what you are doing, or vice versa. Make sure all proprieties are met.

Squash

To see squash in a garden indicates a need for patience in achieving your goals. To see something squashed warns you not to antagonize anyone, especially your superiors, lest you would suffer badly.

Squirrel

To see squirrels in your dream denotes a pleasant surprise, as well as favorable business conditions. To dream of having a squirrel for a pet means happiness and contentment. To kill a squirrel signifies a lack of tact on your part.

Stable

To dream of being in a stable that is sparse but clean suggests something with humble beginnings will have wide-reaching effects. This is an encouragement to believe in yourself.

Stadium

To see a stadium full of people cheering is a sign of great

encouragement for whatever you have in mind. If they are booing, however, it suggests you will not find support.

Stage Coach

To dream of riding in a stage coach denotes a rough period where others are in control and making your life difficult.

Staggering

To dream of staggering indicates strong opposition to your wishes, or burdens that are too heavy for you to carry.

Stags

To dream of stags implies that you have many true friends and your power behind the scenes is in much demand by gatherings and organizations.

Stain

To dream of a stain suggests your thoughtless behavior creates unpleasantness.

Stairway

To see a stairway suggests progress in life and career, not without effort, but with assistance from others along the way.

Stale

To see stale food or coffee means you have outmoded ways of interacting with others, which gives no satisfaction to either party. This is encouragement for you to change.

Stallion

To see a fine stallion in your dream implies that you will achieve honor and riches. To dream of riding a gentle stallion portends you'll gain much distinction locally.

Stamps

To dream of stamps denotes you need to make behind-the-scenes communications in order to clear a situation.

Stapler

To dream of using a stapler signifies that diverse thoughts or items need to be brought together firmly.

Starching

To dream of adding starch to a man's shirts or clothing suggests that you are entering a more formal period of your life. At this time, observing rules carefully will be very important. If starch is being added to a woman's clothes, it implies that she will gain importance in reputation, position, or both.

Star of Bethlehem

To dream of this magnificent star or of the event it signifies is an omen of much promise and goodwill. Do not hesitate to follow your ideals or dreams; providential assistance will be with you.

Stars

To dream of seeing clear and brilliant stars tells of good news, prosperity, and pleasant trips. Shooting or falling stars, on the other hand, mean that sorrow lies ahead.

Starving

To dream of seeing others in a starved condition implies problems and financial difficulties. To dream that you suffer from starvation means unexpected good fortune.

Statues

To dream of sculptured figures denotes that a gift will come from someone you thought had lost all respect for you.

Stealing

To dream of catching a women in the act of stealing and holding her until a police officer arrives, but through her smiling and innocent expression the officer refuses to arrest her and sets her free, indicates that you will reveal a secret of your past life that someday you will greatly regret. To dream that you have stolen something, and afterwards are discovered with stolen property, but you return it to the owner and all is forgiven, denotes that you will receive unexpected money. To accuse others of stealing denotes that you lack consideration toward others in your actions. To dream of something being stolen hints that you should question what values are important to you, and you should hold fast to them.

Steam

To see steam suggests a lot of strong emotions, and anger will ensue. To take a steam bath indicates you need to open up more to others.

Steamboat

To see a steamboat suggests you are using outmoded methods to achieve your aims.

Steel

To see an object of steel in your dream foretells that you will encounter someone of importance who will be of benefit to you. If you attempt to bend a steel object and do so successfully, steel refers to a challenge that you'll overcome with ease. But if you fail to bend the object, circumstances will remain unchanged, and you are advised to rethink your position.

Steeple

To dream of seeing a high steeple on a church implies an uncertain physical condition, a warning to the dreamer of an illness. To dream of climbing a steeple, and to succeed in reaching the top, means success and honor. To fail to reach the top portends many difficulties of various kinds.

Steps

To dream of walking up steps is a very good sign. It denotes you will better your situation in life and achieve honors. In relationship matters it indicates a happy union, and that together, by industry, you will achieve the life you desire.

Stick

To dream of a large stick in the hands of another, which appears threatening, is a signal to beware of alienating someone in authority. If you are waving the stick, or using it in a threatening manner, it suggests a need to assert yourself more, but not necessarily in an overly aggressive manner.

Stillborn

To dream of a stillborn birth relates to discouraging incidents and many things to distract your attention from the regular work routine.

Stilts

To see others walking on stilts means uncertainties in business conditions. To walk on stilts yourself denotes opposition from others relating to a plan that you have proposed to them for their approval.

Sting

To feel the sting of an insect in your dream implies unhappiness due to rigid demands from others.

Stockings

For a woman to dream of beautiful stockings denotes that she is fond of admiration and encourages men's attention through her actions. To see her stockings torn denotes that she will do whatever is necessary to gain financial reward. This is a warning to resist temptation.

Stocks

To dream of buying stocks implies that investing in something, whether a stock, a talent, or time in a project, will bring returns. To sell a stock hints that it is time to cut your losses with something that is at a standstill or is backtracking.

Stomach

To see a flat, strong stomach implies you have guts, or should display such courage in dealing with an issue. To see a flabby, round one suggests you may be getting lax in habits or responsibilities. To see a pregnant woman's belly predicts success and joy with a new project or idea.

Store

To dream of a large store filled with goods indicates success through rapid advancement. To dream of being in a large store portends pleasure and good fortune. To dream of working in a store means your success is brought about through your own personal efforts and hard work.

Stork

To dream of a stork that is flying suggests that the birth of a child will soon be announced. To dream of two storks signifies a happy and fruitful marriage.

Storm

To dream of hearing the howling of a storm, and if the storm causes destruction, indicates business troubles and disagreements with friends. Should the storm pass by without causing any damage, the above indication will be greatly improved and your outlook better.

Stove

To see a tempting meal cooking on a stove signifies that your life will be successful and that the fruits of your labors will help many. If a meal or dish is burned or inedible, it implies that your activities are neither timely nor well received by others, and thus denotes disappointment.

Strange Behavior

To see yourself or someone else do something crazy but harmless, denotes a need to be yourself despite others' opinions. To act silly in a dream, with others not approving, suggests your behavior needs to be synchronized more with the standards of those around you. To see yourself or someone else act in a truly crazy manner that scares you indicates that a weakness or bad habit you have could get out of control and cause you harm; you are advised to deal with it before it becomes a problem. But to act silly amid laughter and approval denotes spontaneity that is encouraged and brings joy to all.

Stranger

If you see a stranger in a dream, think of two negative qualities that you believe he or she displays. Then ask if either of these adjectives applies to you, at least in terms of a present situation, but not necessarily as a permanent characteristic. Generally, a stranger is a reflection of your own qualities.

Strangling

To dream of someone being choked implies that you, or

someone important to you, is holding back important communications due to fear or circumstance. You are advised to invite communication in a comforting manner. If the dream shows someone choking on food, it is a warning that your eating habits need attention and, if left unchanged, will result in health problems.

Straw

To dream of bundles of straw in neat rows signifies abundance and prosperity, and a time of rest soon to come. However, if the straw is scattered about in a dingy, uninviting setting, this suggests that you need to complete unresolved issues or business before prosperity can enter.

Strawberries

To dream of strawberries tells of success in love and a happy marriage. To eat strawberries means honor and security in business.

Street

To dream of wandering in a street aimlessly denotes mental anxiety, and that you may become discouraged with your job. To dream that you are walking the street in a happy mood means that your desired goal will be realized. To dream of being on a dark street and to experience fear, although you are not molested, denotes that you will achieve great success after your strenuous efforts.

Stripes

To dream of clothing or decorations that are striped suggests a need to bring order to a project or circumstance that will ensure its success. If the stripes are vertical, you will gain much by this success, both personally and socially. If the stripes are horizontal, you will advance something that society greatly needs.

Struggling

To dream that you are engaged in a struggle means that difficulties to overcome lie ahead. To dream of coming out victorious signifies success due to your firm determination.

Studying

To see yourself or someone else studying hints that something around you needs to be examined in depth. If you are planning to embark on a course of study, it is a strong encouragement to do so.

Stuttering

To dream of stuttering signifies a fear or anxiety in communication, likely because something important needs to be communicated, but you are afraid to do so. The dream is an encouragement to express yourself, nevertheless. To stutter and then speak eloquently denotes a current shortcoming that will later turn out to be a great strength.

Success

To dream of achieving success, whether great or small, is a wonderful omen. It implies a fine achievement, if you persevere in your undertakings. However, if you envy the success of another in a dream, this suggests that your own anger and resentment are impeding your success.

Suffocating

To dream that you are suffocating implies sorrow due to the coldness and indifference of someone you deeply love. To see others suffocating means you are being imposed upon due to your kind nature.

Sugar

To dream of eating sugar denotes that you will experience things that are not as pleasant as you imagined they would be, but your perseverance will help you in working toward your goal.

Suicide

To dream of suicide denotes that your reserved and self-centered tendencies cause people to misjudge you. To see another commit suicide means that others' losses and reversals of fortune may directly affect you.

Sun

To dream of the sun is always considered a good sign for those who have problems, or for those who must deal with their enemies. To dream of seeing a bright sun denotes the discoveries of secrets for the growth of business. To see the sun rise means good news. To see the sun setting portends false news pertaining to losses.

Sunday

To dream it is Sunday denotes a need to rest and to explore your spirituality and inner self.

Sunflower

To dream of a large, beautiful sunflower suggests that by sharing your talents you will help many and accrue benefits.

Sunstroke

To dream of sunstroke suggests you are letting yourself be overexposed to something, either an activity, a person, or a set of beliefs.

Surgical Instruments

To see surgical instruments in your dream denotes worry and outlay of money due to illness, and predicts accidents that may occur in the family.

Surprise

To dream you are pleasantly surprised predicts that opportunity will soon knock at your door. If the circumstance is unpleasant, it is a warning that something you are counting on will unexpectedly fall through. If you are doing the surprising, and it is received politely, you are about to achieve a breakthrough regarding a long-cherished hope.

Swallows

To dream of these harbingers of summer is a very favorable

omen. They denote a period of prosperity, joy, and rest soon to unfold.

Swamp

To dream of a swamp suggests hidden health problems that should be investigated. If, however, you are in good health, it implies that confusing and strained emotions will lead you toward your own undoing. In this case, you are advised to let go of or cut yourself off from the circumstance that is causing confusion and pain.

Swan

To dream of large and beautiful white swans on clear and quiet waters foretells prosperity and pleasant occurrences. To dream of black swans on muddy and troubled waters means that pleasure will bring disgrace and loss of reputation.

Swearing

To dream of hearing others swearing indicates obstacles in business. To lovers, swearing means interferences in their love life.

Sweating

To dream of sweating profusely speaks either of a need for physical activity that will clear out your system, or it denotes great anxieties that you will soon face. If the dream ends well, you will overcome them.

Sweeping

To dream of sweeping your bedroom indicates a need to give

your spouse or loved one more attention. If the kitchen is being swept, eating habits need to be reexamined, for present habits will lead to decreased energy. If an area of work is being swept, this denotes that a merited increase in responsibilities and position is imminent.

Sweetheart

To dream that your sweetheart has a pleasant and good-natured personality indicates that your marriage will be a happy one, not filled with yelling or arguments. To dream of a sweetheart who is unpleasant and opinionated means happiness will vanish and an end to the relationship is probable.

Sweets

To dream of happily eating sweet things signifies an invitation for fun, merriment, and socializing that will soon come to you, and will bring great joy. If you are eating sweet things but feel remorse, guilt, or unhappiness as you do so, this is a warning to eat less of these foods. If you see sweets and long for them, but do not eat them, this denotes loneliness and a need to open yourself up to new activities and relationships.

Swelling

To dream of seeing a foot or leg swelling suggests that you should take care in career and financial matters, because, unbeknownst to you, something seeks to thwart your success. To dream of a hand swelling is a warning not to be greedy in a financial transaction or speculation.

Swimming

To dream that you are swimming in clear water with skill and ease speaks of success in your business. To dream of swimming under water, or that you bob up and down, portends struggles and humiliations.

Swinging

To enjoy the back-and-forth motion of a swing foretells upcoming sexual pleasures. To swing leisurely and happily predicts a carefree, relaxing period to come.

Sword

To dream of wearing a sword is good; it relates to distinction. To dream that a friend hands you a broken sword indicates trouble with the law, where your defense will be ignored and you will receive little or no compassion. To dream of seeing many swords points to differences to be resolved.

Synagogue

To dream of this house of worship suggests that you will meet with obstacles that you will overcome. This experience will ultimately bring great spiritual rewards.

Syringe

To dream of a syringe filled with a deadly substance like heroine or poison is a warning not to get involved with someone who presents something as wonderful that in fact will bring disaster.

T

"Men have conceived a twofold use of sleep; it is a refreshing of the body in this life, and a preparing of the soul for the next."

JOHN DONNE, English poet

Tabernacle

To dream of this hallowed temple of God indicates spiritual advancement and a great blessing that can be used to help others.

Table

To dream of a table full of appetizing foods denotes the indulgence of pleasures. To dream of clearing a table implies pleasures that will wind up in difficulties. To dream of eating from a table portends happiness and comfortable circumstances. To dream of breaking a table means disappointment.

Tablecloth

To see a clean, white tablecloth foretells a formal, joyous event. To see an ornate or embroidered tablecloth suggests that past efforts are about to come to fruition. If a tablecloth is soiled, it warns not to let personal shortcomings or grievances mar something special.

Tacks

To dream of tacks on a bulletin board signifies ideas and thoughts that need to be worked out more clearly. To see tacks on a floor warns of difficulties with people around you; they need to be handled carefully lest you be the loser.

Tail

To dream of seeing the tail of an animal implies annoyance over trivial things. To dream that you possess a long tail similar to that of an animal foretells a gloomy outlook relating to a new project. To dream of cutting a tail means that you should think before you speak tactlessly in public.

Tailor

To dream of a tailor measuring your body for clothing implies pleasant surprises ahead. To dream of a tailor at work denotes confusion connected with your duties. To have trouble with a tailor points to small losses of some kind.

Talisman

To dream of receiving this type of a charm means profits due to the honest advice of a friend. For an unmarried woman to dream of receiving a charm indicates that her lover has decided she is the only one for him.

Talking

To dream of someone who acts as if he wants to talk with you, but doesn't, denotes that nothing will become of a seemingly good idea. To dream that you are talking to others denotes worrying prematurely. To hear people talk, or to feel that they are talking about you, predicts that you will be accused of contributing to the downfall of another.

Tambourine

To dream of seeing others using this instrument, or hearing its sounds, denotes pleasant surprises mixed with a gradual increase in business. To dream of dancing to one means great delight is yours to enjoy.

Tapestry

To dream of seeing beautiful tapestries denotes culture and refinement, and that you are extravagant in your taste. To dream of possessing a tapestry means wealth will be acquired. For an unmarried woman to dream of tapestries indicates a brilliant marriage.

Tapeworm

To dream of suffering with a tapeworm denotes that you are nervous, restless, excitable, and let imagined illness influence you needlessly. To see a tapeworm signifies disappointment.

Tar

To dream of having tar on your hands or on your clothes

denotes disappointments and irritations. To see it in large quantities means troubles caused by enemies.

Target

To see a round bull's-eye target suggests you need to set your sights clearly, and practice something.

Tarts

To dream of baking tarts foretells that an event or gathering you are planning will be joyous. To dream of happily eating tarts suggests attending a social function in the near future that will provide beneficial contacts.

Task

To dream of completing a task that has been boring or burdensome implies that a period of servitude in career or relationship is about to end. If the completed task gave you joy and you regret its ending, this signals the need to move on into new life circumstances, even though you do not feel ready to do so.

Tasting

To taste something sweet foretells a pleasant experience. To taste something bitter warns of sad news and outcomes.

Tattoo

To dream of seeing someone tattooed denotes that the success of others will hurt your feelings and minimize your abilities. To see yourself tattooed implies family separations.

Taxes

To dream of being unable to meet your taxes, or that you feel they are too high, denotes that you will be excessively pressured to fulfill an obligation. To pay taxes and feel satisfied denotes hopes to be realized.

Tea

To dream of tea in general denotes financial difficulties that are a drain on your assets, which are worrying you. To drink tea portends pleasures that will create problems. To see others drink tea means you will be asked to help someone in trouble.

Teaching

To dream you are teaching young ones suggests that you have highly developed talents that need to be shared with others. To dream of teaching peers, or those who are older, denotes acknowledgment for your achievements and talents, and honors that were long in coming. If the dream contains a scene of a teacher who attempts to force knowledge upon others, it suggests that you back away from a circumstance in which you are involved, because your talents will not be appreciated.

Teapot

To pour from a teapot suggests others will gather about you to receive your advice and opinions, which you can freely give.

Tears

To dream of shedding tears suggests you will soon confront a situation that will deeply affect you. Or, that someone around you is hurting inside but hiding it, and needs all the consolation you can provide. To dream that you are overcome by emotion with crying indicates sorrow. To see others in tears means others will be sympathetic to your suffering.

Teasing

To dream of teasing another means that your friends think that you are clever and come to you for advice. To dream of being teased means that joy, contentment, and future popularity lie ahead for you.

Teeth

To dream of having false teeth and taking them out of your mouth implies dental work that will be either painful or unsatisfactory. To dream that your teeth are worn down to the gums denotes quarrels with a close associate that will end in disgrace. To dream that your teeth are loose portends unpleasant things to cope with. To lose teeth predicts that hardship will rob you of your pride. To have teeth examined is a warning to be careful of enemies. To dream of having poor teeth indicates money troubles. To spit teeth out denotes illness and sorrow in the family. To dream of one tooth being longer than the others suggests pain caused by a parent. To have a tooth fall out points to sad news. To dream that your teeth are white and beautiful, when, in reality, they are not, means joy, health, and prosperity. To dream that your teeth are so long that they annoy you portends quarrels and possible lawsuits.

To dream of teeth, in general, relates to how you communicate and what effect your communications have upon others.

If the teeth are clean and beautiful, you communicate successfully and it brings good fortune. If the teeth are decaying, you communicate poorly, and it turns others against you. If a tooth is broken, you are warned that you are missing some communication that is important to an enterprise. If teeth are falling out, you are advised to stay silent for a period of time because your communications are too profuse and are no longer effective. To dream of a gold tooth suggests you will have an idea that, if communicated to others, will bring good fortune.

Telegram

To dream of sending a telegram predicts that you will have difficulties with a very close friend who, in turn, will criticize your business. To dream of receiving a telegram is an indication that you will receive profitable news.

Telephone

To dream of talking on the telephone denotes rivals, both in business and in love.

Tempest

To dream of a tempest implies controversies with friends; misfortune is also predicted. To dream of being knocked down by a tempest denotes malicious planning among your enemies.

Temptation

To dream of resisting temptation means trouble of some kind.

If you succeed in resisting temptation, success will come after much hard work.

Tent

To dream of a city of tents signifies changes in region. To dream of being in a tent means a change in business. If the tent is strong and secure, the change will be good.

Terror

To dream of being terrorized by something denotes disappointment. To see others terrorized indicates sad news from friends.

Test

To dream of taking a test indicates there is something you need to prepare for. However, if you have actually been studying for a test or a major exam, the dream may mirror your anxiety, or it can be a practice session for taking the actual exam.

Thanks

To give thanks in a dream suggests you will receive the help you have been seeking. To receive thanks means that you can help another and should do so.

Thaw

To dream of seeing ice thaw relates to pleasure and profit. To dream that it is thawing from beneath you denotes energies directed in the wrong direction.

Theater

To dream of being in a theater relates to pleasant and congenial friends. To dream that you are an actor in a theater denotes an early change in your situation, which will prove profitable. To dream of being in a theater during a fire signifies a change that will not be profitable.

To dream of entering a theater is an omen of something dramatic that will soon cross your path. If you are an actor on a stage, this shows that you are losing touch with your true self and playing too much of a role in life, imposed by others. If you are in the audience in the dream, and enjoying a play, this suggests you should sit back quietly and remain an observer amid changes in some area of your life, such as family or career.

Thief

To dream of thieves entering your house and robbing you denotes profit and honor. To dream of catching a thief and arresting him indicates shrewdness on your part in deceiving your enemies. To dream that you yourself are a thief signifies you are being careless with moral or material things that you value, and you should remain firm and careful. If you are a thief being chased by the police, this denotes business troubles.

Thighs

To dream of admiring your thighs indicates pleasure and good cheer. For a young woman to admire her thighs predicts that her foolishness and selfishness may cause her to make wrong decisions, resulting in unhappiness. To dream of muscular and well proportioned thighs suggests that you have strength and are successfully enduring the journey of life; it will bring you success. If the thighs are weak, thin, or unsightly, you are proceeding through life in a negative manner that will result in a negative outcome.

Thimble

To use a thimble in a dream signifies a small matter that will need your attention, but which should be handled very carefully.

Thirst

To feel thirsty in your dream denotes that you are very ambitious and love leadership. To dream of quenching your thirst means your love for leadership will be rewarded or that great emotional satisfaction will soon be yours. To suffer from thirst in a dream suggests an unfulfilled need that you are not in touch with, and should examine.

Thorns

To dream of seeing thorns denotes that your neighbors are envious toward you. To dream that thorns are on your body means you will be harassed. To dream of being pricked with thorns portends troubles with the dreamer's employment. Any thorn in a dream is a warning of unexpected antagonism from another. To dream of a crown of thorns predicts great suffering that you will need to accept with patience and resignation. To see a thorn on a rosebush hints that there is a price to pay to achieve something beautiful and wonderful.

Thread

To dream of a thread whose source is not seen denotes a mystery that you will not unravel. To thread a needle in a dream is a signal that you need to pay more attention to minute details in order to successfully complete something. To see a tangled thread suggests that lies or deceptions you perpetrate will come back to haunt you. To dream of tangling it yourself means you will tell a secret to an indiscreet friend and it will become public knowledge. To dream of unraveling a thread denotes discovery of a secret.

Threshing

To dream that you assist in threshing a huge amount of grain denotes joy and a prosperous business. To see others threshing means you will enjoy great pleasure from the generosity and wealth of others.

Throat

To dream of cutting another's throat denotes that you will injure a person accidentally. To dream that your throat is cut means hopes and success will be shattered. To dream of a well developed throat means success will be achieved in the near future. To dream of having a sore throat indicates anxiety. To see a beautiful throat suggests that some communication you make will benefit you. If someone attempts to grab your throat in a dream, it implies that another is trying to influence your thinking, and that person should be avoided.

Thunder

To hear thunder in your dream is a warning that troubles will endanger your business. Hearing thunder in a dream can also signify rumors and unsettling conditions that will get your attention and could create fear; however, if you stay calm, it will pass without affecting you. To hear thunder while seeing vivid lightning flash indicates loss of wealth.

Tibet

To dream of this land of wise and mysterious inclinations portends an inner journey that will astound you.

Ticket

To dream of buying a bus, train, or airplane ticket suggests an urge to start something new. If you board, this foretells you will begin the venture. If you do not board or do not reach your destination, it is not yet the time for change.

Ticket Agent

To dream of interacting with a ticket agent suggests you lack something that is needed to progress in your career or life. To receive a ticket suggests you will overcome this lack.

Ticking

To dream of hearing a clock ticking is a signal that you need to speed up with whatever responsibility or talent you have been developing. Doing so will enable you to take advantage of an opportunity that is pending but still unknown to you.

Tickle

To see someone tickled and laughing heartily indicates release from tension soon to come.

Tidy

To see things tidy and in place denotes either a need to be more orderly in fact or in thought. Or, if the scene is too meticulous, this suggests you need to be less obsessive about details.

Tie

To see a man putting on a silk tie signals advancement. To see a wool tie denotes a reliable and trustworthy person.

Tiger

To dream of a tiger denotes jealous and furious enemies. To succeed in warding off a tiger indicates efforts to be achieved. To kill a tiger means complete success.

Tin

To see a tin cup or utensil forewarns poor quality in workmanship or goods.

Tipsy

To dream that you are tipsy denotes that you are very optimistic and take life as it comes. To dream of seeing others tipsy denotes that you are too thoughtless of the future.

Toad

To dream of toads portends misfortune of some kind. To kill

a toad implies that you are too impetuous and reckless. To play with one means you will be misjudged by a friend.

Toast

If you are eating toasted bread in a dream you will have reason to feel satisfied because some accomplishment will be recognized. To dream you are giving a toast at a gathering or ceremony signifies that you will soon have reason to rejoice.

Tobacco

To dream of tobacco is a happy omen. To dream of smoking tobacco foretells much pleasure. To chew tobacco means good news is to be expected. To see tobacco grow denotes success in business.

Toenails

For a woman to dream that she is painting her toenails predicts that a new or old love interest will be rekindled shortly.

Toes

To dream that your toes itch foretells a journey you will soon take. This may be an actual trip or a journey of the mind, as you learn new things or take on a creative project.

Tomatoes

To dream of tomatoes is a good omen. To dream of eating tomatoes indicates splendid health. To gather tomatoes means happiness in marriage. For unmarried people to dream of tomatoes portends a happy marriage in the future.

Tomb

To see a tomb in a dream denotes regrets. To help build a tomb portends birth of children. To fall into a tomb indicates sickness and misery in the family. To read the inscription on a tomb means you'll have to perform duties that are unpleasant.

Tongue

To dream that you see your tongue, or that your tongue is very large means that you are misunderstood and accused of something you did not do. To dream of seeing someone else's tongue predicts you will hear gossip maligning your character.

Tools

To dream of tools that are in good shape suggests talents or skills that you are not using, but should.

Toothache

To dream of a toothache may be a warning of an actual infection that is building. Consider whether a dental checkup is due. If your teeth are healthy, the dream suggests other hidden conditions, that, unbeknownst to you, are becoming troublesome.

Top

To dream of playing with a child's toy top indicates that you are wasting your time with something or someone, and going around and around in circles. It implies the situation is best dropped.

Torch

To dream of holding a burning torch is a good sign, for it

signifies accomplishment and eventual acclaim. To see a torch extinguished or darkened signifies disappointment in cherished activities or circumstances.

Tornado

To dream you are exposed to a fierce tornado that threatens you with destruction warns of overwhelming circumstances that may soon overtake you. However, this is avoidable by letting go of the potential source of trouble, such as a relationship or a job situation.

Torpedo

To dream of a torpedo signifies a shocking discovery.

Torture

To dream that you assist in torturing others denotes that plans you thought favorable will prove unsuccessful. To dream of defending others from torture portends success after much hard work. To dream that you are tortured yourself implies sorrow due to the actions of deceptive friends.

Tour

To dream of taking a pleasant tour in a foreign land denotes new horizons, as actual journeys or as new projects. If the tour shows many things speeding by, this implies you may be too superficial in your life.

Tower

To dream you are ascending a tall tower denotes that you are in a period of adversity, undergoing challenges and reversals of fortune. Eventually, you will recover to a state of comparative affluence and ease.

Town

To dream you see towns filled with people, merchants, and hustle and bustle, denotes a life filled with constructive activity, and is a favorable omen. However, if the town is dismal and the people have unhappy faces, this signals that you should not make changes that are being contemplated in some area of your life.

Tradesman

For a man to dream of a tradesman implies that he should let his ambitions rest for a while and be satisfied with the work that is presently before him. It signals that currently he is not in a period of opportunity for career advancement.

Tragedy

To dream of a tragedy denotes friends and wealth. To dream that you contributed to, or were involved in, a tragedy, implies personal miseries and profound regret.

Train

To dream that you are riding on a train implies good news relating to a contemplated project. To dream of attempting to board a train on time, but just missing it, denotes that present complications will ultimately prove beneficial to you. To dream of being on top of a train, and that you reach your destination successfully, portends achievements and prosperity. To drop off a train, or to fail to reach the desired destination, indicates disappointments and irritations.

Tramp

To dream of a tramp or street person is a signal that taking pity on the plight of others will benefit you.

Trap

To dream of catching game in a trap denotes success. To dream of being caught in a trap means enemies will succeed in their plans. To set a trap yourself implies that your plans or deceptive actions will be discovered.

Traveling

To dream of traveling on foot denotes a great deal of hard work lies ahead. To dream of traveling by horse-drawn carriage portends profit and pleasure combined. To dream of traveling by train indicates hopes to be realized. If traveling by water, this indicates prosperity and happiness. To dream of traveling pleasantly without incident denotes favorable conditions.

Treasure

To dream of finding hidden treasure suggests unused, hidden talents that could bring you happiness and success in life. If treasure first appears to be real gold or precious jewels, and then is seen to be fake, this warns that some offer or prospect before you will lead to naught.

Trees

To dream that you are climbing a tree and reach the top easily means that you are lucky. To fail indicates an obstacle to cope with. To fall from a tree means misery and sickness. To see green trees portends hopes to be realized. To cut a tree down suggests the senseless spending of money.

Trial

To dream of witnessing a trial foretells a period where you are under scrutiny by others, which creates tension and stress. To be a jury member at a trial indicates a need to cooperate with others in order to reach a decision on a serious matter.

Tricks

To dream of seeing tricks performed denotes fun and happy surprises. To dream of card tricks, and that you can detect the trick, means business matters will improve.

Triplets

To see triplets in your dream foretells that your judgment is good, and is a warning for you to continue with your plans.

Trophy

To dream of trophies that you have won, or that were presented to you, implies an achievement gained through pleasant and courteous behavior.

Trousers

To dream of trousers refers to secrets which may never be

revealed to you. To dream that you put trousers on inside-out denotes forming an attachment that will be hard to resist.

Trumpet

To hear the blowing of a trumpet denotes startling news that is nearby. To blow a trumpet yourself indicates ambition to be achieved.

Trunk

Trunks, as a rule, are related to trips. To dream of packing your trunk means you are soon to make a trip. To dream that your trunk is too small predicts you are to be promoted shortly. To see your clothes scattered all over the trunk, instead of being placed inside, indicates you will go to a place that will dissatisfy you, and that you will return, sorry you left in the first place.

Tuba

To see a large tuba refers to work or talents that others reject, but which will benefit you.

Tube

To see a tube connecting two items signifies that openness will create solutions in work or in a relationship.

Tugboat

To see a tugboat denotes someone in a humble position will be of assistance to someone in a high position.

Tug-of-War

To see this game played in a dream is a signal of friendly competition that benefits all.

Tulip

To dream of this floral harbinger of spring predicts a change for the better arriving in your life.

Tumbleweed

To dream of a tumbleweed denotes an urge to set down roots and to find security.

Tumor

To dream of a tumor is a signal of something building up behind the scenes that needs to be detected and removed. Ask questions and review that which is your responsibility, lest unforeseen problems overtake you.

Tune-up

To dream of bringing a car or vehicle in for a tune-up hints that you should do so for your car, or possibly that a medical checkup would be due. If both car and body are in good shape, then there is a need to examine habits and add something invigorating for mind or body.

Tunnel

To dream of going through a tunnel while on a train indicates an illness and a possible change in business. To dream of being in a tunnel and meeting a train foretells unhappy conditions relating to business. To dream of being in a tunnel, and to meet with difficulties there, is always a bad sign.

Turban

To dream of someone wearing a turban suggests mysterious conditions or persons will communicate something important.

Turkey

To dream of a turkey strutting about suggests that you examine current actions to estimate if they are wise. To dream of a turkey being prepared for a sumptuous meal indicates the beginning of a bounteous period.

Turnips

To dream of seeing a large turnip patch means that circumstances will soon improve. To dream of eating turnips foretells mild illness for the dreamer. To prepare a dish made with turnips means that success due to your self-made abilities is imminent.

Turpentine

To dream of seeing turpentine means unhappiness in the near future. To dream of using turpentine on someone for medical purposes denotes those whom you've helped owe you a great deal of gratitude.

Turtle

To see this shy creature is a hint to continue on your path despite great obstacles; success will ultimately be yours.

TWINS

Turtleneck Sweater

To dream of a sweater with a high neck is a signal to be more reserved and perhaps guarded in your communications. Do not tell all, at least for a while.

Twilight

To see twilight in a dream denotes something coming to a natural end.

Twins

To dream of healthy twins means business success and many happy hours at home. To dream of sickly twins means sorrow and unhappiness.

U

"Dreams are but interludes that fancy makes...
Sometimes forgotten things, long cast behind
Rush forward in the brain, and come to mind."

JOHN DRYDEN, English poet

UFO

To dream of an unidentified flying object suggests that ideas you have, or which are presented to you, must be carefully examined to make sure they are not too strange. To dream of alien beings emerging from a spacecraft indicates feeling distant from others, or of meeting someone who is strange.

Ugly

To dream of being ugly signifies misunderstandings between loved ones. In business, things are inclined to drag. For a woman to dream of being unattractive signifies that her cold and indifferent actions will cause her friends to think much less of her.

Ulcer

To dream of having an ulcer portends many worries.

314

Umbilical Cord

To see the umbilical cord of a newborn baby being cut suggests that a new idea or project is ready to be put into action. To see one on yourself, or on an adult that is attached to another, implies that you or someone close to you needs to establish independence.

Umbrella

To dream of umbrellas means that petty problems will ultimately come to a head and annoy you very much. To dream of lending one means destroyed confidence. To borrow one means you will distrust a friend, which will ultimately bring about an end to your friendship. To dream of having the storm turn an umbrella inside out denotes irritations from others who want to belittle your reputation.

Umpire

To see an umpire making a call at a baseball game indicates your work or actions will be judged. If the umpire indicates a player is safe, you will be judged favorably.

Uncle

To dream of your uncle relates to unpleasant news. To dream of seeing your uncle suffering or in a bad situation denotes family quarrels.

Uncoordinated

To see yourself or someone else's limbs move in an uncoordinated way signifies you are trying to do too many things at once. If your career or life direction is not on track, you need to take a long-term view and develop a career plan so as to reach your best potential.

Underdog

To see someone as the underdog suggests you are feeling sorry for yourself, or that you or someone else needs help to escape an overpowering circumstance.

Undergarments

To see a man's undergarments suggests a need for strength. If you are already strong in character, it implies a new power-fulness that will bring you forward in life. To see a woman's undergarments suggests a need for gentleness and kindness. If others observe your underwear, it hints you may be feeling vulnerable and that you reveal too much of yourself to others.

Undergraduate

To dream of being an undergraduate in college indicates you need to recall what you learned early in life, because those lessons will stand you in good stead now. However, if you have not been to college, it suggests that developing your skills through courses or studies will benefit you.

Undertaker

To see an undertaker signifies an unexpected change, which can be either dire or wonderful. It signifies death if someone has been ill or very unhappy.

Undress

To dream of seeing others undress denotes that your joy and satisfaction will end in an uncertainty. To see yourself undress denotes that you will learn bad reports about yourself. For a woman to dream of undressing in the presence of others denotes that lies regarding her conduct will annoy her greatly and cause her much dismay.

Unemployed

To see someone unemployed, but not distressed, in a dream hints at a change in responsibilities; but this will occur smoothly. To see an unemployed person greatly distressed foretells a change in career or work that is disruptive and unpleasant. Because fate will lead you to something better, it's best not to fight it.

Unicorn

To dream of this mythical creature signifies great fortune. It is an omen of talent, intuitive abilities, and guidance from seen and unseen forces.

Unicycle

To dream of pedaling a one-wheeled bike denotes unusual skills that will gain the attention of others, but which will require independence to develop.

Uniform

To dream of wearing a uniform denotes distinction in your vocation or career. For a young woman to dream of wearing a uniform implies a wealthy and happy marriage.

317

Upholstery

To see beautiful fabric on a sofa or chair foretells new aspects in your home life that will bring you great joy.

Upper Class

To dream of someone in the upper class acting in a benevolent and kind manner signifies help from those in a higher position, and that you may occupy such a position in the future. If this person acts in a snobbish or degrading manner, it warns not to look to one in power for help.

Uptight

To see someone very rigid and stressed out who acts strangely because of anxiety hints that you should not let present worries and circumstances get the better of you.

Urgent

To dream that you are helping the continuance of an urgent appeal predicts involvement from which you may have some difficulty removing yourself.

Urn

To dream of urns denotes that you will turn a struggling business into great success, much to the surprise of others. If they are broken, expect troubles in business.

Ushering

To dream of someone ushering another to their place is a signal that you will soon find your niche in life or career.

318

Usurper

To dream that you are seizing or holding property illegally denotes that you will have trouble over possessions, or in establishing good credit. To dream that others are usurping your rights implies keen competition in business that will test your skills in learning how to win.

"The net of the sleeper catches fish."

Greek proverb

Vacation

To dream of taking a vacation you enjoy denotes less stressful times in your future and a respite from problems.

Vaccination

To dream of seeing others vaccinated denotes that you are too easily led by flattery and seldom think until it is too late. To dream of being vaccinated yourself denotes that the finger of suspicion will be pointed at you, and it will be difficult for you to prove your innocence. For a woman to dream of being vaccinated on the leg denotes lies regarding her character are being told by others.

Vacuuming

To dream of vacuuming suggests you must exert yourself to gain control of whatever you need. It also suggests that you need to hold back negative thoughts and communications.

Vagrant

To dream of seeing vagrants denotes fear from a report of illness in the community. To help or feed a vagrant denotes many happy returns. To dream that you are one yourself denotes obstacles and annoyances to overcome.

Valedictorian

To see a valedictorian or to be one in a dream denotes accomplishment that will be applauded by many.

Valentine

To dream of receiving a valentine denotes disappointments relating to the heart. To send them means that you will let good opportunities slip through your fingers.

Valise

To dream of finding a valise denotes prosperity. To lose one means sorrow and many struggles in reaching your goal.

Van

To dream of a large van suggests you have much to do in life.

Vanilla

To see a vanilla ice cream cone foretells fun and relaxation of a traditional nature. To add vanilla flavoring to a dish being cooked denotes that something needs a boost of energy or a good word to make it acceptable.

Varicose Veins

To dream of varicose veins signifies a difficult path in life.

Varnish

To see others varnishing in your dream means irritations through the interferences of others in your daily duties. To do varnishing yourself means that your thrifty and economical qualities are highly appreciated by your superiors.

Vase

To dream of a beautiful vase denotes many happy conditions will surround you in your future. To dream that you drop a vase and break it denotes shattered hopes relating to business plans. For a woman to dream of receiving a vase as a gift implies that her ambitions will be achieved and rewarded.

Vat

To see a vat full of wine denotes prosperity; to see one full of water denotes the need to practice moderation for a period of time.

Vault

If you dream of a vault, some influence will cause you to examine what is closed up in you emotionally. If the vault contains valuables, such an examination will release deep feelings that will offer much joy and peace. To dream of a vault containing money signifies that your conduct and way of living puzzles many, and has them wondering about you. To dream of a vault for the dead indicates sad news and things going wrong in general.

Veering

To dream of turning off the road or path suddenly is an omen of an unexpected turn of events, but it need not be negative.

Vegetables

To dream of eating vegetables is an indication of unstable conditions. You may think that you are on solid footing, and all of a sudden, things may go in an opposite direction. These uncertainties are generally caused by those you sincerely trusted. To dream of rotting vegetables denotes disappointments. To dream of preparing them for a meal implies that success will come gradually, but surely.

Vehicle

To dream that you are thrown from a vehicle means that gossip will irritate you and that you will stop at nothing to find its source. To ride in a vehicle successfully and without suffering from any mishap denotes that you will be victorious over resistance caused by others.

Veil

To dream of a veil in general denotes that you are not as sincere with friends as you might be. To dream of losing a veil means a disagreement with a man. To see a bridal veil in your dream denotes a change that will be lucky. To dream of weaing a bridal veil predicts an affair that will be completed successfully. To dream of mourning veils means disappointments and troubles.

Veins

To dream of seeing bleeding veins denotes sorrows and troubles that will not end.

Velvet

To dream of velvet is a happy omen; it predicts much happiness to the dreamer. For an unmarried woman to dream that she is wearing a velvet dress denotes many suitors will love her and ask her to marry them.

Vendor

To see a sidewalk vendor selling foods or goods suggests you will have an opportunity, but you must take it swiftly when it appears.

Vengeance

To dream of taking vengeance warns you to forgive and forget, lest ill befall you.

Ventriloquist

To dream that you are a ventriloquist denotes that people distrust you and are afraid to deal with you. To dream of listening to a ventriloquist denotes that you must be more careful of what you say in public.

Venus

To see a statue or picture of the goddess of love hints that love will enter your life, but you must seek it.

Vermin

To dream of seeing vermin crawling about means worries due to sickness. To dream that you succeed in exterminating them denotes victory in an attempt at a goal.

Vest

To wear a vest in a dream hints at a rise in status.

Vice

To dream that you are encouraging vice in any form denotes that you are in danger of losing your reputation.

Victim

To dream that you are a victim of another's clever actions denotes that others will seek to injure you. To dream that you victimize another implies wealth gained by questionable manners.

Victory

To dream that you are victorious in any contest denotes that you will outsmart your enemies to their great surprise.

Video

To dream of renting a video indicates a need to put aside daily struggles for a while and relax. To buy one suggests a need to incorporate a regular habit or regimen of rest and relaxation.

Villa

To dream you are admiring a villa situated in some picturesque and pleasant location signifies that you are in need of a period of rest or a vacation. The opportunity to take one may soon cross your path.

Vine

To dream of creeping vines is a happy omen. If they contain blossoms, the sick will recover and those in good health will be more rugged and vitalized. To dream of vines that are poisonous means a rundown vitality should be taken care of in order to avoid unhappiness.

Vinegar

To dream of vinegar in general denotes difficulties or obstacles of some kind. To dream of drinking it means worries and duties to perform that are not pleasant.

Vineyard

To dream of being in a vineyard with all its ripe fruit denotes joy as a result of a successful investment. To the lover, it predicts an early marriage. To dream of a vineyard with fruit that is out of season is not a lucky sign.

Violets

To dream of violets is a splendid sign. For an unmarried woman to gather them denotes that she will soon meet her future husband. To dream that you gather great quantities of them means fame and riches.

Violin

To dream of seeing someone playing the violin and that the music is harmoniously sweet denotes to the businessman that pending investments will turn into unexpected good fortune. For an unmarried woman to dream of playing music on a violin means that her aspiration will be achieved to the height of her ambition.

Virgin

To dream of a virgin is very lucky; it denotes success in many directions. For an unmarried woman to dream that she is no longer a virgin denotes that she will jeopardize her reputation by becoming or acting too intimate with male associates. For a married woman to dream that she is still a virgin denotes that certain conditions will bring about her past and will cause regret. When a man dreams of seducing a virgin, this predicts that his plans relating to the development of business will be slow.

Visions

To have someone that you know appear in a vision relates to troubles in your family. To dream of having strange and confused visions confront you denotes an illness.

Visit

To dream that you are visiting is a happy omen; more so if the visit has been pleasant. To dream that a friend is visiting you portends good news from someone you like. To dream of receiving a visit from someone who appears in distress means struggles and disappointment.

Vitamins

To see vitamins in a dream suggests either your body or your morale needs a boost.

Vodka

To dream of a bottle of vodka suggests a trip to a faraway place, but beware of losing your valuables while there. To drink from a bottle of vodka suggests unbridled instincts. If you are too reserved, this is a hint to let go.

Voices

To hear calm, pleasant voices in your dreams denotes pleasure and contentment. Should the voices be unpleasant or angry, disappointments are signaled to the dreamer. To hear crying voices is a warning to be careful of what you say in a fit of anger.

Volcano

To dream of an erupting volcano means differences that have to be resolved. The dreamer should be very careful after such a dream regarding what is said to those with whom you have differences.

Volleyball

To dream of a volleyball game signifies a happy circumstance of cooperation by which all benefit, but this will not advance you personally.

Voluptuous

For a woman to see a woman of beauty and much appeal in a dream hints that unfolding her feminine charms would be appropriate. If a man dreams this, it indicates a desire he should seek to fulfill in a constructive manner.

Vomit

To see others vomiting in your dream denotes that you will be harassed by lies about you. To dream that you are vomiting implies that there is danger of an illness for you.

Voodoo

To dream of such rituals is a signal you or others around you are misusing energies, which can do harm.

Vote

To dream of voting denotes a petition in your community on which your signature is solicited. To dream of being paid to vote a certain way, or for a certain party, means that you will take a step against your better judgment.

Vow

To dream that you see someone making any sort of vow denotes a complaint in regard to the handling of your affairs. To dream of taking a vow, or making a vow yourself, foretells deceit and delusion.

Voyeur

To see a voyeur in a dream hints that either you or someone close to you is treading where they should not, which should be discouraged.

Vulgar

To see vulgar actions or hear vulgar words spoken in a dream signals rudeness from others. If you are the rude one, this could backfire and bring unhappy consequences.

Vultures

To dream of vultures generally refers to prolonged illnesses, sometimes to enemies that are trying to harm you.

"But I, being poor, have only my dreams."

W. B. YEATS, Irish poet

Wading

To dream of wading in clear water denotes joy and pleasure is certain to be yours.

Waffle

To see a plate of waffles suggests that business dealings are uncertain and should be questioned. If you eat a waffle, ask yourself whether you are being direct enough in a communication or dealing, lest you lose out.

Wager

To dream of betting denotes that you will resort to cheating in order to make your plans succeed. To lose a wager implies that illegal actions are being committed by those who dislike you.

Wages

To dream of receiving wages means a change to your advantage. To dream of an increase in wages portends profitable undertakings. To have them reduced indicates unpleasant things from those you once highly respected.

Wagging

To see a dog wagging its tail denotes loyal friendship and support. To see someone wag a finger warns that what you say or do could cause trouble, unless you are careful.

Wagon

To dream of a wagon warns of dissatisfaction in general. To dream of getting into a wagon means shame due to an unfortunate accident. To dream of getting out of a wagon portends loss and a possible struggle to keep what is rightfully yours. To dream of riding down a hill means hope to be furthered. Riding uphill signifies discouragement relating to work. To drive over an embankment implies sorrow and grief. To dream that you are driving very close to the edge of a cliff denotes some illegal involvement over which you will be very annoyed, and from which you must disassociate yourself.

Waif

To dream of a waif suggests you are spending too much time alone.

Wailing

To dream of hearing someone grieve or wail in sorrow suggests the need to be more sensitive to the pain of others. Or, it may predict news that will bring sorrow.

Waiter

To dream that a waiter is pleasantly serving you denotes happy hours spent in the presence of friends. To see one who gives poor service and is grumpy means that you will be bored by friends.

Waiting

To dream of waiting for something denotes unclear goals or the need for patience.

Waking Up

To dream of waking up is a signal that you are blind to something that requires attention.

Walking

To dream that you are walking and rejuvenated denotes consolation and happiness. To dream of walking and to find it difficult to continue implies troubles and pain. To walk at night implies struggles and complications, as well as danger from unexpected sources, particularly while traveling. To dream of walking during the day indicates you should make an effort to be more observant to what is going on around you.

Wall

To dream of coming to a wall and being unable to pass denotes difficulties in convincing others of your way of thinking. To dream that you jump over a wall means you will be able to overcome all obstacles and reach your ambition. To dream that you are walking on top of a high wall with perfect ease foretells success in your business in the future.

Wallet

To dream of finding a wallet with money denotes good fortune. To find an empty one indicates worry and problems.

Walnut

To dream of walnuts is a happy omen. To dream of opening walnuts, or eating them, means difficulties followed by wealth and satisfaction. To dream of gathering them portends discovery of a treasure.

Wallpapering

To put up attractive wallpaper suggests that the past can be left behind by filling the present with positive experiences.

Waltz

To dream of waltzing with someone you like suggests that you are attaining peace of mind. A partnership may follow that will bring success in business or love. To dream of waltzing with someone you dislike or abhor suggests the need to let go of grievances against another.

Wandering

To dream of wandering about suggests the need to review life goals. If you have no clear-cut ambitions, it would be advisable to set some. If you already have goals that are so clear-cut as to be inflexible, this is a warning to let up and go with the flow.

Want

To dream of seeing others in want or need implies dissatisfaction in services rendered by others. To dream that you are in want or need denotes that you are too thoughtless of the future; you should form a plan for steadily increasing your savings for the future.

War

To see a war going on in your dream denotes arguments within your immediate family. To dream that you are in a war denotes persecution. For a young woman to dream that her sweetheart is going to war means scandal relating to a close friend.

Wardrobe

To dream of having a large, splendid wardrobe denotes profit and rapid strides forward. To dream of having a poor wardrobe means that you are displeased with your community and the people around you.

Warehouse

For a young person to dream of acquiring a warehouse and filling it with goods denotes success in a business direction. For a businessperson to dream that a warehouse is on fire or is broken into by thieves suggests that a loss could take place unless certain directions are changed.

Warts

To dream of seeing warts on your person means an annoyance, or that you are unable to get out of a certain thing or affair. To dream of seeing warts on others is a sign of unknown enemies around you. To see a wart on a finger or hand implies that some responsibility is being avoided or dealt with poorly.

Washing

To dream of washing denotes that some personal interest will suffer through misjudgment. To dream of washing your body or face means that you may have to forget your pride to ask for a certain thing or a favor.

Wasp

To dream of wasps denotes enemies that are trying to malign you. To dream that they sting you means you will be very annoyed to learn what your enemies have done. To dream of a wasp any time is an omen of ill will from a friend or toward a friend; careless words could bring a sting to the relationship.

Waste

To dream of much being wasted and discarded warns of overlooking important items, which will lead to distress. You are advised not to take things for granted and to express your appreciation.

Watch

To dream that you break a watch denotes that trouble is ahead of you. To see watches in your dream relates to successful investments. To dream of receiving a beautiful watch portends pleasant recreations and an upcoming period of accomplishment. To dream of any watch or clock is also a warning to be careful how you spend your time, lest some opportunity pass you by.

Water

To dream of seeing clear water is always good. To dream of being in or on turbulent waters denotes a disappointment relating to a deal. To dream of crossing a muddy stream means troubles collecting money that is owed to you. To dream of throwing small stones into water so clear that you see them sink to the bottom denotes that you will receive something that you have been anxiously awaiting. Muddy water always foretells gloom and disappointment. To dream of seeing water rise so high that it comes into your house denotes a great struggle in resisting something immoral. To dream of falling into water that is muddy predicts that you will suffer from many mistakes. To dream of drinking water that isn't clear foretells sickness. To dream of drinking clear water indicates health.

Waterfall

To see a nice clear waterfall in your dream denotes that your ambitions will be realized and that you will live in wealth in years to come. To dream of a waterfall is always a very favorable omen, foretelling an abundance of goodwill, generosity, and opportunity in your future. If there is a rainbow at the bottom of the waterfall, this benefit comes after a lengthy period of work and effort.

Watermelon

To see a large watermelon denotes relaxing and refreshing moments to come.

Waves

To dream of seeing clear waves denotes pleasure and the accumulation of wisdom. To see waves that are muddy and choppy indicates losses from poor judgment.

Waving

To dream of waving to someone indicates a need to get someone's attention. Or, waving hints that you are missing someone else's signals.

Wax

To see something made of wax suggests that whatever is being considered is not permanent. Seeing wax figures as in a wax museum is a warning that some people in your life pretend to be what they are not and act in a two-faced manner. If you yourself are the figure in wax, this indicates a weakness that needs to be confronted and overcome.

Wealth

To dream of wealth, or to see others wealthy, denotes the sincerity of friends that would help you should you have financial problems. To dream that you are very wealthy predicts that your stamina and aggression will help you attain your goal. For an unmarried woman to dream that her associates are wealthy implies that she has high ideals, and that there is a good possibility of having them realized.

Weaning

To see small animals being weaned by their mother is a signal that you need to grow up and prove yourself in your own circumstances.

Weapon

To dream of brandishing a weapon and warding off something dangerous is a signal that you need to assert yourself and take the offensive to resolve your situation. If, however, the aggression in the dream is bloody and lays waste to much amid great agony, this warns you to find a peaceful, nonaggressive solution to a problem, lest you lose everything.

Weasel

To dream of a weasel suggests someone will try to get out of a commitment or responsibility. Let it not be you.

Weather

To dream of sunny and beautiful weather is a good omen, predicting success and happiness on whatever issue concerns you. To dream of severe rain and storms denotes a period of trials and tribulations, which will pass. To dream of bleak, cold weather implies that you do not feel loved and that you need to change something, either within yourself or in your life, in order to receive it. To dream of snow piled high suggests the need to withdraw from activities for a while as a renewal.

Weaving

To dream of trouble-free weaving indicates your painstaking

efforts will prove rewarding. If accidents occur while weaving, such as the ends entangling or the loom breaking, struggles in your undertakings lie in the future. To see others weaving predicts favorable conditions will surround you.

Wedding

To dream of a wedding foretells an early approach of discontent and bitterness. To dream that you are married secretly suggests discovery of gossip attacking your character. To dream that there are oppositions to your wedding denotes jealous rivals.

Wedding Clothes

To see wedding clothes in your dream, whether they are the bride's, groom's, or attendants' garments, denotes that you will sincerely and pleasantly perform your duties, and that you will meet new and interesting friends.

Wedding Ring

To dream of a wedding ring denotes that your future life will be a pleasant one with very little change or unhappiness.

Wedlock

For a woman to dream that she is unhappy in her marriage denotes that she will hear many disagreeable things, and that others have a compulsion to watch her too closely. To dream of divorcing denotes disappointment, grief, and many petty jealousies.

Weeds

To see a lawn or area filled with weeds suggests bad habits that hold back your progress. To weed a garden or lawn denotes steps are being taken to improve something.

Weeping

To dream that you are crying generally brings sad news or upheavals in your immediate family. To dream of seeing others cry denotes hope and joy, after many controversies. To the unmarried, to dream of weeping means that there are troubles in love to be suffered.

Weighing

To dream of weighing yourself on a bathroom scale suggests that you are neglecting eating habits. To dream you are weighing an object signals the need to carefully weigh the value of a decision you are about to make, or of an item you are about to acquire, lest it not match your expectations.

Weight Lifter

To see someone lift weights suggests that work which will be demanding, and which you would at times like to avoid, will give you skills that will later empower you.

Welcome

To dream you are welcomed is an encouragement to proceed with a relationship or a venture.

Welcome Mat

To see a welcome mat in a dream suggests you can proceed with confidence.

Well

To dream of standing by the side of a well in the country suggests resources of strength and sustenance that you can call upon in time of need, for self and others. This implies that you possess gifts of healing that can be used for the good of all.

Wet

To dream of being wet is often a warning to take care of your physical welfare, since exposure or overheating may cause illness. For a woman to dream of being wet to the skin means trouble and disgrace that can result from being in an illegal relationship.

Whale

To dream of seeing a large whale causing destruction denotes struggles and possible loss of property.

Wheat

To dream of seeing wheat in its ear denotes profit and wealth for you. To see wheat in large quantities portends great wealth. To see large fields of wheat indicates encouraging prospects. To see wheat in sacks means ambition will be achieved. To see wheat in a granary, but diminishing gradually, suggests that enemies may be plotting to harm you.

Wheelbarrow

To see a wheelbarrow suggests that you use an old or ancient technique, method, or skill to go forward.

Wheelchair

To dream of a wheelchair denotes something important is not working, which you may not be aware of. Or, a wheelchair suggests that emotionally you or someone close to you may be in need of healing.

Wheels

To stare at rapidly moving wheels in your dream denotes success in business and that family matters will resolve themselves. To set or fix broken wheels relates to some disappointment in business matters.

Whip

To dream of a whip or hear the cracking of a whip points to difficulties and many things that need resolution.

Whirlpool

To see a whirlpool in your dream predicts troubles in business and that the dreamer will suffer from mental stress. If the whirlpool is dirty, it indicates that enemies may cause problems.

Whirlwind

To dream that you are caught in a whirlwind denotes that you will not like the change that will take place soon.

Whiskey

To dream of whiskey in any form denotes that you will push your selfish tendencies so far that your friends will dislike you. To dream of drinking whiskey indicates many struggles before you reach your desired goal. To see others drinking whiskey suggests money gained through much scheming.

Whistle

To dream that you are whistling denotes that you are looking forward to an event centered around you, and where others will criticize you unjustly. To hear others whistle predicts that you will be opposed in a prospective plan by friends who are playing a joke on you.

White

To see something in pure white denotes a fresh, new beginning.

Whittling

To dream of cutting chips away from a piece of wood is an indication that taking small steps toward something will build into the end result you seek.

Widow

To dream of being a widow denotes troubles and many annoying things being said by others. For a man to dream that he marries a widow means shattered hopes and forestalled ambition will cause him sorrow. To dream of a widow dressed in black is an omen of loss. This may be a loss of something cherished or of a loved one. For a woman to dream that she has become a widow is a signal of a need to become more independent.

Wife

To see your wife in your dream denotes domestic troubles, generally due to jealousy on the part of your wife. To dream that your wife is lovable and agreeable indicates success in business. To dream of fighting with your wife, or abusing her, means there is cause for your wife's suspicion. For a husband to dream that his wife is in the embrace of another man means a disappointing business proposition will be presented.

Wig

To dream that you are forced to wear a wig due to the loss of hair predicts that you will be influenced to make a change that you will regret. To see others wearing wigs implies you are being wished bad luck.

Wild

To dream that you are turning wild means misfortune through some careless act. To see others in a wild state indicates mental disturbance and senseless conditions.

Wild Beast

To dream of a wild beast suggests that you are exhibiting its qualities. If the animal shows positive qualities, you also possess the same qualities. However, if the wild animal wreaks havoc and carnage, your attitudes, words, or actions are out of hand, and need to be controlled.

Will

To dream of making your will denotes depression and problems. To dream that a will is made in someone else's favor instead of yours indicates quarrels of a shameful nature. To dream that you make a will and then destroy it predicts that there is trouble coming, which should surface soon.

Win

To win at some game denotes triumph over difficulties and good fortune in a career.

Wind

To dream that you hear gusty winds blowing loudly predicts anxieties and mental stress caused by competitors. To dream that wind keeps blowing you backwards indicates disappointment relating to some cherished hope.

Windmill

To dream of seeing a windmill denotes the attainment of honor, an influential position in your community, and wealth.

Windows

To dream of open windows denotes secret schemes right under your nose. To see windows closed means you will be denied something you desperately want. To dream of jumping through a window predicts trouble nearby. To dream of slipping in through a window suggests the possibility of a lawsuit.

Wine

To dream of drinking fine wine with friends shows power and fortune. If you are drinking alone, this suggests loneliness and a need to improve your social life. To dream of uncorking a bottle of champagne hints you will have a very special cause for celebration. To uncork a bottle of wine foretells good times with loved ones. However, if what is uncorked is sour or declined in quality, this hints that something that once was wonderful may turn sour.

Wings

To dream that you have wings and are able to fly denotes that you take and shoulder the troubles of others too often; consequently, you worry needlessly too much.

Wink

To see someone wink indicates someone will share a secret, an invitation, or proposition with you. Or, someone will secretly propose an invitation or deal; if the wink happens in a positive context, accept it; otherwise, refuse it.

Winter

To dream of winter, when in reality that is not the season, denotes that the dreamer will encounter a slight loss. This minor loss will be brought about through the suffering of a mild illness, from which the dreamer will fully recover in a short period of time.

Wire

To dream of being caught or entangled in a wire denotes that others are afraid of you because you are so stern. To see a rusty wire in your dream denotes troubles due to an uncontrollable temper.

Wishbone

To dream of a wishbone indicates something you would like—but are afraid—to express to others. To dream that you pull on a wishbone, and get the larger portion, predicts you will obtain your wish if you do what is necessary.

Witch

To dream of witches denotes that a lull in business is causing you dissatisfaction, and that you are searching for opportunities to improve conditions.

Wizard

To see an individual who claims to work wonders in wizardry in your dream denotes that you will be annoyed, not only in business, but in public affairs as well.

Wobbling

To see an object wobbling warns that something is not as secure as you thought it was; it needs to be checked out.

Wolf

To dream that wolves are following you while you are driving, but that they are unable to harm you, fortells of success in business. To dream that you kill a wolf foretells that those whom you trust will deceive you by failing to make good on promises given. To see a pack of wolves means you love to win through sharp scheming.

Woman

To dream that you quarrel with or slap a woman denotes a disappointment in someone you desperately wanted to meet. To dream of seeing a woman hiding warns that an unprincipled person is taking advantage of your good reputation by passing himself off as your associate. To dream that a woman is watching you denotes that a former misunderstanding will be straightened out. To dream of committing adultery means that the person you were once intimate with will cause a lot of problems. To see a pregnant woman predicts receiving pleasant news. If the dreamer is a man, to see a woman with a beautiful figure indicates joy and satisfaction; for a woman, this dream means jealousy, arguments, and scandal. To dream of seeing a woman quarrel portends disappointment.

Wood

To dream you are cutting or chopping wood shows you will be happy in family life and prosperous and respectable in your career. To dream of chopping or sawing down a tree and yelling "timber" as it falls denotes that the fruits of past actions are about to come to you. If you have been acting positively and constructively in your life, the results will be positive; but if you have shirked your duties to self or others, the results will be negative. To dream of carrying wood suggests that success will come through perseverance and industry. To dream of sitting in a wooded area by a stream suggests the need to review your life to decide what is truly important.

Woodworm

To dream of a woodworm denotes that your present condition is but temporary. You are advised to build for the future beyond today's transitory pleasure.

Wool

To dream of seeing wool means slow but sure prosperity, and that you will attain influential prominence in your community. Should the wool be in unusable condition, this foretells of differences that will not coincide with others, and you will be called stubborn.

Work

To dream of seeing others at work denotes money gained after hard work and concern. To dream that you are at work yourself denotes success after having tried many different things, for past experiences have forced reality upon you.

Worms

To dream of seeing worms on or near your body denotes little ambition, lack of self-reliance, and easily discouraged characteristics. To dream of killing them predicts that you will determine to build character in this direction. To use worms for fishing purposes means you will make some sudden gain greatly to the surprise of friends.

Worshipping

To dream of worshipping in a holy place suggests that retaining your spiritual roots and ideals will bring benefits and the answers you seek.

Wound

To dream of seeing others wounded predicts an injury or actions taken to hurt you by seemingly good friends. To have a wound yourself means business troubles and many things will annoy you.

Wreath

To dream of a wreath that is fresh and pretty denotes success and prosperity. To see a wreath that is withered predicts illness or unhappiness caused by loved ones.

Wrecks

To dream of seeing a wreck denotes many distressing obstacles and setbacks in business, and that you may need to seek another career.

Wren

To dream of this little bird is a good sign because the wren is known for its innocence. It indicates you are surrounded by noble friends.

Wrestling

To see wrestling by professionals foretells career hassles. To see spontaneous wrestling between two people suggests aggression and anger that will result in outbursts, unless you control yourself.

Wrinkles

To see wrinkles on someone's face suggests wisdom and honor. But to have wrinkles and feel anguish means you are resisting the acceptance of a mature path and actions.

Wrist

To see a wrist in a dream warns of a need for flexibility. If the wrist is broken, it suggests that rigidness will lead to dire consequences.

Writing

To dream that you see others write denotes accusations from those you tried to please. To write yourself denotes a miscalculation that will probably cause a loss in business. To read writing warns you to watch those who are trying to interest you in new schemes.

X

"Was it a vision, or a waking dream? Fled is that music:—Do I wake or sleep?"

JOHN KEATS, English poet

X-Ray

To dream of having an X-ray taken of your teeth or other part of your body foretells of a mysterious occurrence in the life of one of your friends. If you dream of looking at your own bones by means of an X-ray, you will be called on to account for an indiscretion you have committed.

Xylophone

To dream of playing a xylophone or hearing one played in a dream is a sign that you will take part in a pageant of historical interest. If the xylophone is played out of tune, it foretells an accident.

Y

"And God came to Laban the Syrian in a dream by night, and said unto him, Take heed that thou speak not to Jacob either good or bad."

GENESIS 31:24

Yacht

To dream of seeing a yacht denotes optimism and foresight, and that your efforts are strengthened, or reinforced with recreation. To see one in distress denotes that business concerns compel you to disappoint friends who are planning a vacation.

Yard Stick

To see or use a yard stick in your dream denotes that your exacting ways are disliked by others and because of this, you are often ignored.

Yarn

To dream you are working with yarn and experience difficulty in untangling it predicts some slight irritation due to disappointments. To handle yarn successfully means success in whatever you may attempt. For a young woman to dream of yarn denotes that her lover greatly respects her.

Yawning

To dream of seeing others yawn means unpleasant conditions and even illness to the dreamer. To yawn yourself denotes that you are restless, nervous, and never satisfied with your life.

Yearning

To have a yearning in a dream indicates a search for something that is lacking, which needs to be pinpointed and pursued.

Yell

To emit a yell in your dreams means that you will be discovered in an unworthy plot. To hear the yell of another is a sign that you will be of help to an old friend in the near future.

Yielding

To see someone yield in a dream and feel good about it, suggests that giving something up or giving up on something will actually be beneficial, rather than a failure.

Yoga

To dream of someone doing yoga indicates gentle exercise would help you find inner peace and strength.

Yogurt

To dream of eating yogurt suggests that acquiring healthy habits or adhering to existing ones is a good idea. Likely you have begun to stray from them.

Yoke

To dream of wearing a yoke of any kind is a sign that you will do hard labor under an exacting taskmaster. To dream of seeing a yoke of oxen foretells a new address quite distant from your present place of abode.

Young Man/Young Woman

To see yourself as the young man or young woman you once were indicates the need to muster strength and use qualities you had in your youth in a present circumstance. To observe a young man in an action that you admire indicates inner strength, and that you should take the initiative in a situation. To see a young woman suggests a need to get more in touch with your feelings and intuitive side.

Youth

For an elderly person to dream of his or her youth denotes continuing ease and comfort.

Z

"To all, to each, a fair good-night,
And pleasing dreams, and slumbers light!"

SIR WALTER SCOTT, Scottish writer

Zebra

To dream of seeing a herd of zebras denotes that you are wasting time and energy on something that will prove harmful to you. To dream you see a zebra that is tame, or that you pet one, denotes profits from a source that will delight you and result in much joy.

Zephyr

To dream of soft zephyrs relates to sentiment. It warns that you will sacrifice a great deal for the one you love and let sentiment interfere with business. For an unmarried woman to dream that she is depressed by zephyrs denotes petty uneasiness and restlessness.

Zigzag

To dream of taking a back-and-forth route toward something suggests you are feeling caught between two things, and must decide between them. Or, it may suggest that an indirect route or mode of communication toward a goal, rather than a direct one, would be more beneficial at this time.

Zinc

To dream of zinc portends good luck to the dreamer. Business will soon climb to a paying basis, resulting in an increase in cash flow. The dreamer may enjoy many benefits and luxuries due to this extra income.

Zipper

To dream of fastening one's clothes with a zipper is a sign that you will preserve your dignity in the face of provocation to do otherwise. If you dream of a zipper getting stuck, you will be chagrined by the actions of one of your friends.

Zodiac

To dream of seeing or studying the system of the zodiac predicts fame and riches to the dreamer through his love for wisdom and charity.

Zombie

To see a zombie in a dream warns of thoughtless actions or words.

Zoo

To dream of looking at animals in a zoo foretells that you will travel to far-off places. To dream of taking a child to a zoo means you will make a great deal of money.